ook

NATIONAL GEOGRAPHIC
Reach™

Language • Literacy • Content

NATIONAL GEOGRAPHIC   Hampton-Brown

Acknowledgments and credits continue on the inside back cover.
National Geographic and the Yellow Border are registered trademarks of the National Geographic Society.

National Geographic School Publishing
Hampton-Brown
www.NGSP.com

Printed in the USA.
DB Hess, Woodstock, IL

ISBN: 978-0-7362-7463-0

13 14 15 16 17 18 19   10 9 8 7 6 5

HPS244184

Contents

Unit 3: Amazing Places

Unit 4: Power of Nature

Unit 5: Invaders!

Unit 6: Treasure Hunters

Unit 7: Moving Through Space

Unit 8: Saving a Piece of the World

Name _____   Date _____

Living Traditions

Make a concept map with the answers to the Big Question:
How important are traditions? Write your ideas on the people
in the circle.

Name _____   Date _____

Street Fair

Make a main idea diagram about the photo of a street fair on page 5.

Main Idea Diagram

💬 **Use your main idea diagram to tell your partner about the street fair picture.**

Name _____ Date _____

Family Gathering

Grammar Rules Complete Sentences

A sentence is a group of words that expresses a complete thought.

1. To find the **subject**, ask: *Whom or what is this sentence about?*

2. To find the **predicate**, look for words that tell what the subject is, has, or does.

Read each sentence. Then circle the subject and underline the predicate.

(Carly) drives to our grandma's house. I come on a bus. Our family

gathers for a party. Grandma makes a special meal. My aunts

help her cook. The kids play fun games. The adults

sit around and talk. Everyone has fun together. We all

help Grandma clean up. Then we say good-bye and go home.

Write two complete sentences. Have a partner identify the subjects and predicates.

Name _____   Date _____

Josh Ponte: A Musical Journey

1

Josh Ponte traveled to Gabon to help save gorillas. He learned that the Gabonese have one of the world's oldest cultures. Their music, dance, and storytelling are thousands of years old.

2

Their music sounds like birds and animals in the forest. The villagers sing and dance all day long. It is a tradition that connects the people as they work and play.

3

Many people in Gabon cannot read or write, so they tell stories through music.

Their traditions and lives are connected to each other and to nature. They respect the world around them.

HB
©

Grammar: Simple Subjects and Predicates

Let's Agree

Grammar Rules Subject-Verb Agreement

1. Action verbs that tell about one person or thing end in -s.
    Uncle Ramón plays music.

2. Action verbs that tell about more than one person or thing
    don't end in -s. *All the adults dance.*

1. **Play with a partner.**

2. **Make a card for each subject or predicate below. Place them face
    down. Take turns turning over two cards at a time.**

3. **If the two cards create a complete sentence and the simple subject
    agrees with the verb, keep the cards. If they do not complete a
    sentence, or if the subject does not agree with the verb, turn the cards
    face down. The player with the most cards at the end wins.**

Peter	My grandpa	My cousins	The dogs
eats tamales	sing songs	help Grandma	plays the guitar
Our neighbors	sleeps over	My uncle	enjoy parties

HB

©

Reread and Retell: Main Idea Diagram

Josh Ponte: A Musical Journey

Main Idea Diagram

He was interested in nature.

Pages 12-13:
Ponte went to Gabon.

💬 **Use your main idea diagram to tell your partner what the interview was mainly about.**

Fluency: Phrasing

Josh Ponte: A Musical Journey

Phrasing is how you use your voice to group words together. Use this passage to practice reading with proper phrasing.

Ramona: Why do you think people in Gabon care so deeply about the   13

natural world?   15

Mr. Ponte: I think it is because their traditions and lives are   27

connected to the natural world. The village is like a family.   38

The natural world provides them with everything   45

they need to live. They get their food from nature. They build their   58

musical instruments and homes from natural materials.   65

From "Josh Ponte: A Musical Journey," page 24.

Phrasing

B	☐ Rarely pauses while reading the text.	A	☐ Frequently pauses at appropriate points in the text.
I	☐ Occasionally pauses while reading the text.	AH	☐ Consistently pauses at all appropriate points in the text.

Accuracy and Rate Formula
Use the formula to measure a reader's accuracy and rate while reading aloud.

_____ − _____ = _____
words attempted   number of errors   words correct per minute
in one minute   (wcpm)

P/HB

Name _____   Date _____

Shaped by Tradition

Strategy Planner

Step ❶ What is the author's purpose for writing this biography?

    ❑ to tell a story   **OR**   ❑ to give information

    ❑ to entertain

Step ❷ What is your purpose for reading?

    ❑ for enjoyment   **OR**   ❑ for information

Step ❸ What type of selection are you going to read?

    ❑ **fiction**   **OR**   ❑ **nonfiction**

Do the following:	Do the following:
• Identify the characters and settings.	• Read more slowly.
• Think about what happens and when it happens.	• Identify facts about real people or events.
	• Use photos.

Preview this selection before you read. After reading, talk with your partner about how you used your preview to understand the selection.

Name _____ Date _____

Compare Author's Purpose

Comparison Chart		
	"Josh Ponte: A Musical Journey"	"Shaped by Tradition"
genre	interview	
author's purpose	to inform about Gabon's musical traditions	
stated? yes/no	yes	
If yes, where? If not, how can you figure it out?		

💬 **Take turns with a partner. Ask each other questions about the authors' purposes.**

HB

©

Grammar: Complete Sentences

Is It Complete?

Grammar Rules Complete Sentences

- A **sentence** is a complete thought.

  It has a complete subject and a complete predicate.

- The **complete subject** tells whom or what the sentence is about.

- The **complete predicate** tells what the subject is, has, or does.

Read each group of words. Write *complete* if the words are a complete sentence. If it is not complete, tell what is missing.

1. Sixteen friendly gorillas _missing predicate_

2. Sing while they work _____

3. Young people mix styles of music _____

4. Josh Ponte films people in Gabon _____

5. Some Gabonese people _____

Make each incomplete sentence above a complete sentence. Add a complete subject or a complete predicate.

_____

_____

_____

💬 Tell your partner only one part of a sentence. Have your partner add the missing part to make the sentence complete.

& HB

Name _____   Date _____

Plot of a Story

Work with a partner. Tell each other the story of your first lost tooth.
Make a story map to tell the plot of your partner's story.

Story Map

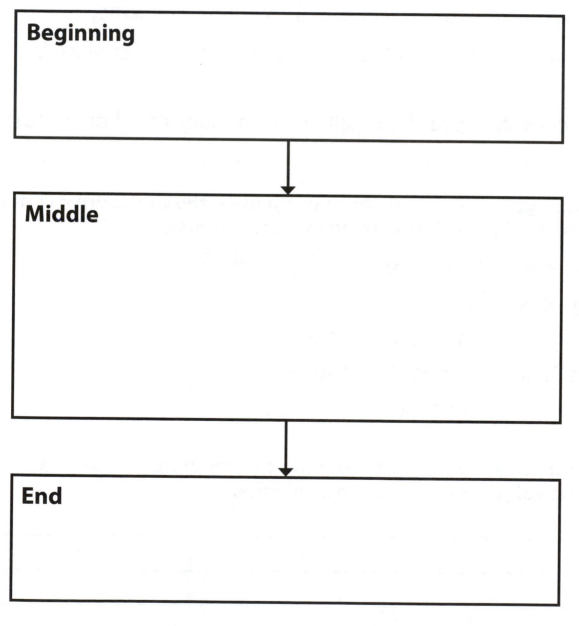

Beginning

Middle

End

💬 **Use the story map to retell your partner's story.**

©   /HB

The Twins' Birthday Party

Grammar Rules Compound Subjects

A compound subject is made up of two simple subjects that share the same verb.

Join the two subjects with *and* or *or.*

The <u>bride</u> (and) <u>groom</u> cut the cake.

<u>Cara</u> (and) <u>John</u> are sitting at my table.

<u>Flowers</u> (or) <u>candles</u> decorate each table.

<u>Adults</u> (and) <u>children</u> dance to the music.

Read each sentence. If the sentence has a compound subject, underline the subjects. Circle the word that joins the subjects.

1. Kara and Kayla are twins.
2. Today is the twins' birthday.
3. Balloons and streamers decorate the yard.
4. Pink plates and cups are on the tables.
5. Grandmother puts candles on the cake.
6. Mom or Dad will light the candles.
7. Kara and Kayla will make a wish.

Tell a partner about a birthday party or other celebration. Use a compound subject in one of your sentences.

Name _____   Date _____

Martina the Beautiful Cockroach

1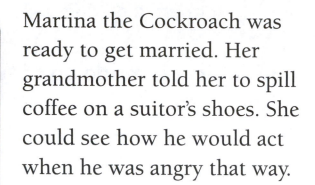

Martina the Cockroach was ready to get married. Her grandmother told her to spill coffee on a suitor's shoes. She could see how he would act when he was angry that way.

2

From the balcony, Martina greeted her suitors—a rooster, a pig, and a lizard. The Coffee Test showed her that they were the wrong suitors.

3

Then Martina saw a mouse and went to meet him. She didn't want to use The Coffee Test for him. Her grandmother said she had to. Martina reached for a cup, but the mouse got one first. He splashed Martina's shoes. She knew he was her perfect match.

Grammar: Compound Predicates

Spin, Create, and Say Aloud

Grammar Rules Compound Predicates

A compound predicate is made up of two or more verbs that share the same subject.

1. Join two verbs with *and* or *or*.

    Suitors visited Martina <u>and</u> asked for her hand in marriage.
    The suitors will <u>either</u> pass the coffee test <u>or</u> fail.

2. Join three or more verbs with commas, plus the word *and*.

    Martina greeted them, smiled, <u>and</u> served them coffee.

1. **Take turns with a partner.**

2. **Spin the spinner. Use the word or words shown or follow the directions to create a sentence with a compound predicate.**

Make a Spinner

1. Put a paper clip 🖇 over the center of the spinner.

2. Put the point of a pencil through the loop of the paper clip 🖇. Make sure it goes through the paper.

3. Spin the paper clip 🖇 to make a spinner.

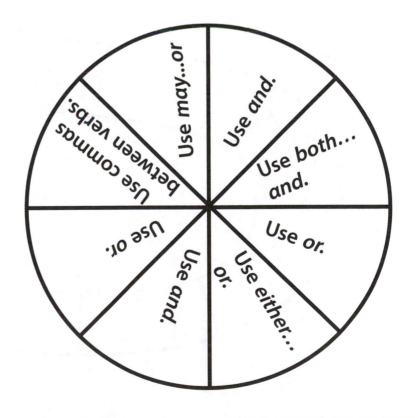

HB
©

Vocabulary: Apply Word Knowledge

Word Race

1. **Play with a partner.**
2. **Write one Key Word on each game board space.**
3. **Flip a coin. Move 1 space for heads. Move 2 spaces for tails.**
4. **Read the word. Tell what it means and use it in a sentence.**
5. **If your partner decides you used the word incorrectly, move back one space.**
6. **The first player to reach the finish wins.**

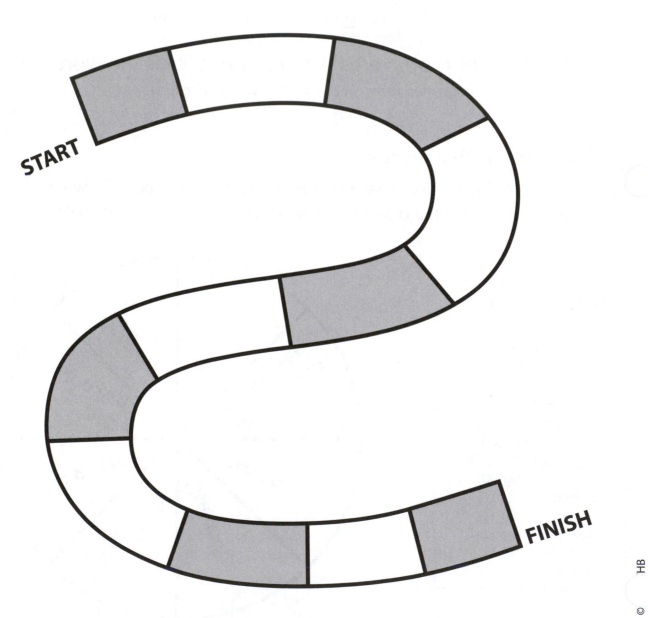

Name _____   Date _____

Martina the Beautiful Cockroach

Complete the story map to tell what happens in "Martina the Beautiful Cockroach."

Story Map

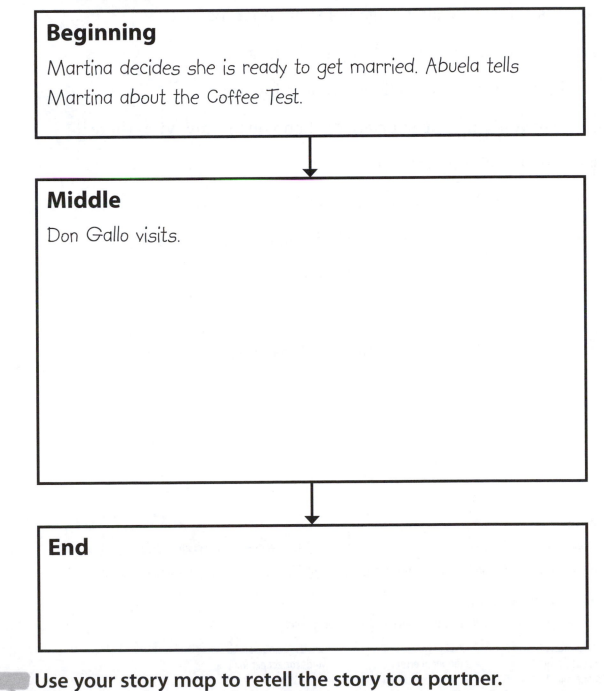

Beginning

Martina decides she is ready to get married. Abuela tells Martina about the Coffee Test.

Middle

Don Gallo visits.

End

💬 **Use your story map to retell the story to a partner.**

Fluency: Expression

Martina the Beautiful Cockroach

Expression in reading is how you use your voice to express feeling. Use this passage to practice reading with proper expression.

"¡*Gronc!* ¡*Gronc!*" squealed Don Cerdo as he dabbed at the   10

coffee on his shoes. "What a tragedy for my poor loafers!"   21

He really is quite a ham, thought Martina.   29

"Calm yourself, *señor*. I'll clean them for you!"   37

"I'll say you will!" he snorted. "When you are my wife, there'll   49

be no end to cleaning up after me!"   57

Martina rolled her eyes in disbelief.   63

"A most charming offer, *señor*," she said dryly, "but I must   74

decline. You are much too boorish for me."   82

From "Martina the Beautiful Cockroach," page 50

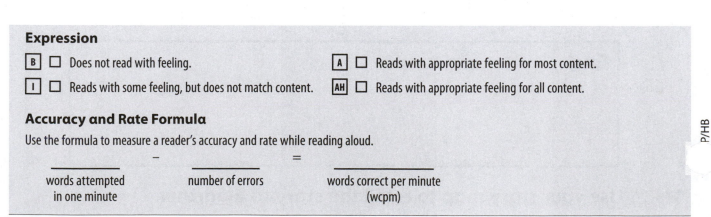

Expression

| B | ☐ Does not read with feeling. | A | ☐ Reads with appropriate feeling for most content. |
| I | ☐ Reads with some feeling, but does not match content. | AH | ☐ Reads with appropriate feeling for all content. |

Accuracy and Rate Formula

Use the formula to measure a reader's accuracy and rate while reading aloud.

_____ – _____ = _____
words attempted   number of errors   words correct per minute
in one minute   (wcpm)

P/HB

Name _____   Date _____

Coming of Age

Complete this log as you read "Coming of Age."

Double-Entry Log

Page	What I read	What it means to me
p. 61	Jyotsna had a special ceremony when she turned eleven.	I will have a quinceañera when I turn 15.

💬 **Tell a partner which detail was most interesting to you and why.**

HB

Name _____ Date _____

Compare Content

Complete the Venn diagram to compare and contrast "Martina the Beautiful Cockroach" and "Coming of Age."

Venn diagram

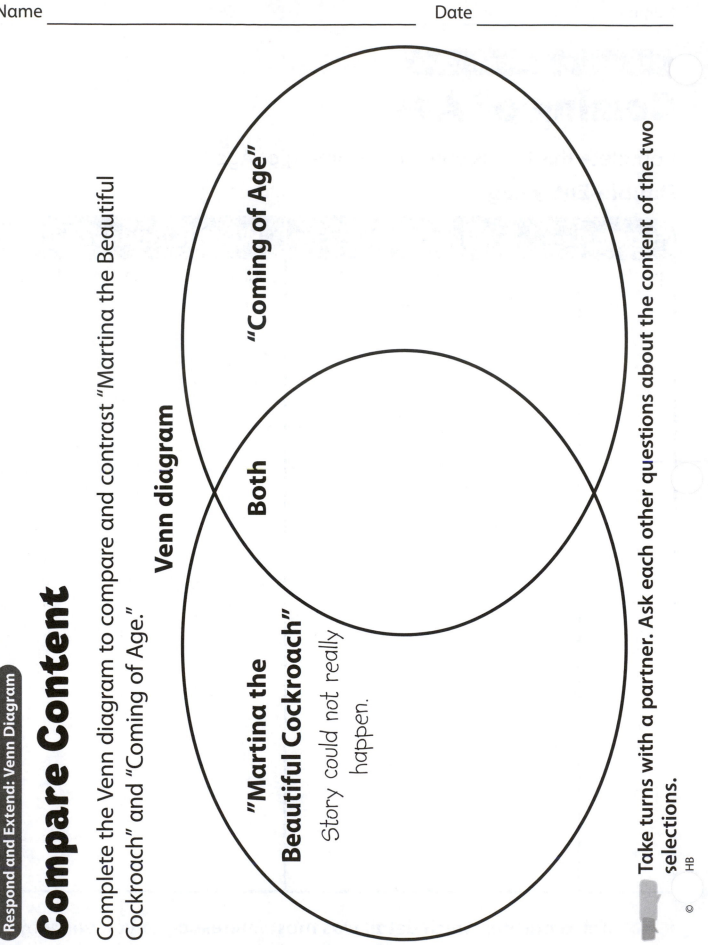

"Coming of Age"

Both

"Martina the Beautiful Cockroach"

Story could not really happen.

Take turns with a partner. Ask each other questions about the content of the two selections.

HB

©

Grammar: Subject-Verb Agreement

Please Agree

Grammar Rules Subject-Verb Agreement

When a **subject** has two or more nouns joined by **and** or **or**, it is called a **compound subject**.

> The **son** and the **daughter sit** on chairs.
>
> Either the **son** or the **daughter sits** on a special chair.
>
> The **son** or the **daughters sit** on a bench.

How do you know what verb to use with a compound subject?

If you see **and,** use a plural verb like *sit*.

If you see **or,** look at the last simple subject.

- Is it singular? Then use a singular verb like *sits*.
- Is it plural? Then use a plural verb like *sit*.

Write the correct form of the verb on the line.

1. My family and I ___celebrate___ important phases in life.
   (celebrate)

2. My best friend and relatives _____ me into adulthood.
   (welcome)

3. My aunt and my uncle _____ my first voni to me.
   (present)

4. My aunts or my sister _____ me gifts.
   (hand)

5. Some women or guests _____ saris to the ceremony.
   (wear)

🗨 **Talk with a partner about special occasions you have shared with other people. Use compound subjects in some of your sentences.**

HB

©

Focus and Coherence

	How do the questions and details fit with each other?	How complete is the writing?
4 **Wow!**	• All the questions and details fit with each other.	• The writing feels complete. • The interview includes a beginning, middle, and end.
3 **Ahh.**	• Most of the questions and details fit with each other.	• The writing feels mostly complete. • Parts of the beginning, middle, and end are clear.
2 **Hmm.**	• Some of the questions and details fit with each other.	• The writing feels somewhat complete. • The beginning, middle, and end are not all clear.
1 **Huh?**	• Few of the questions and details fit with each other.	• The writing feels incomplete. • The interview has no clear beginning, middle, or end. It just has a few questions or answers.

© &HB

Name _____   Date _____

5Ws Chart

Complete the 5Ws Chart for your interview.

Who?	
What?	
Where?	
When?	
Why?	

Name _____   Date _____

Revise

Use the Revising Marks to revise these paragraphs. Look for:

- a strong beginning
- logical order of questions
- sufficient detail
- precise words

Revising Marks

∧	Add.
℘	Take out.
⌒⌢	Move to here.

Chef and Restaurant Owner Lam Phan

Lam Phan sailed across the ocean to the United States. He is the chef-owner of Pho Pasteur, the best Vietnamese restaurant in the area. Diners make reservations weeks in advance to eat his dishes. I asked him about his nice restaurant.

What do you hope to do in the future?

I would like to do more. They would be in different parts of the city.

Then I could share my traditions and fine food with even more people.

What was one of the important things you did when you first opened your restaurant?

I looked everywhere for the perfect things to fill the space.

I wanted diners to be comfortable, and I wanted them to have

the experience of my culture and traditions in my restaurant.

© & HB

Edit and Proofread

Use the Editing Marks to edit and
proofread this paragraph. Look for:

- compound subjects: subject-verb
  agreement
- avoiding comma splices
- spelling compound words

Editing Marks

∧	Add.
℘	Take out.
⬯⟶∧	Move to here.
⬯	Check spelling.

    **Why do you and your staff takes such good care of the people
who eat in your restaurant?**

We want everyone who eats here to feel like part of our family. We
want all the diners who come here to enjoy themselves,   we want
them to come back often. I truly hope they will be customers for ever.

**You have diners who come to your restaurant often,   there are
also many new diners. What can every one expect when coming
to your restaurant?**

All diners can expect excellent food and service, and we will help
new diners get to know our food and traditions. We appreciate and
velcome all of our customers.

Name _____   Date _____

Animal Intelligence

Make a concept map with the answers to the Big Question:
Just how smart are animals? Write your ideas on the bodies of the ducks.

© & HB

Thinking Map: Character Chart

Tell About a Character

Make a character chart about a story you have read.

Character	What the Character Does	What the Character Says	What It Shows

Tell a partner about your character and his or her traits.

Grammar: Kinds of Sentences

The Prickly Porcupine

Grammar Rules Kinds of Sentences

Kind of Sentence

A **statement** tells something.	I went to the zoo.
A **question** asks something.	Where are the penguins?
An **exclamation** shows strong feeling.	I love penguins!
A **command** tells you to do something.	Take a picture of the seal.

Categorize the sentences. Write each sentence under the correct heading.

What is this animal? It is a porcupine. Be careful. It has sharp quills. Those quills can hurt! Do not mess with a porcupine.

Statement	Question	Exclamation	Command
It is a porcupine.			

Tell a partner about a favorite animal. Use different kinds of sentences.

© & HB

Name _____   Date _____

Love and Roast Chicken: A Trickster Tale from the Andes Mountains

1 Cuy the Guinea Pig saw Tío Antonio the Fox and had no time to hide. He told Tío Antonio that the sky was falling. Tío Antonio began to hold up the rock. He got tired and let go. The sky didn't fall. Tío Antonio was angry at Cuy, but Cuy had gone to the farmer's house.

2 Cuy helped the farmer during the day. At night, Cuy ate the alfalfa. The farmer noticed someone was stealing his alfalfa. He made a sticky gum doll. Cuy got stuck to the doll. The farmer found Cuy.

3 The farmer tied Cuy to a tree. Tío Antonio saw Cuy and wanted to eat him. Cuy told Tío Antonio that the farmer's daughter wanted to marry him. Cuy would have to eat roast chicken. Tío Antonio took Cuy's place. When the farmer found Tío Antonio, he told him what Cuy said. The farmer laughed. Tío Antonio escaped. He said Cuy would never trick him again. He stayed far away from Cuy.

Grammar: Different Kinds of Questions

You Asked, Didn't You?

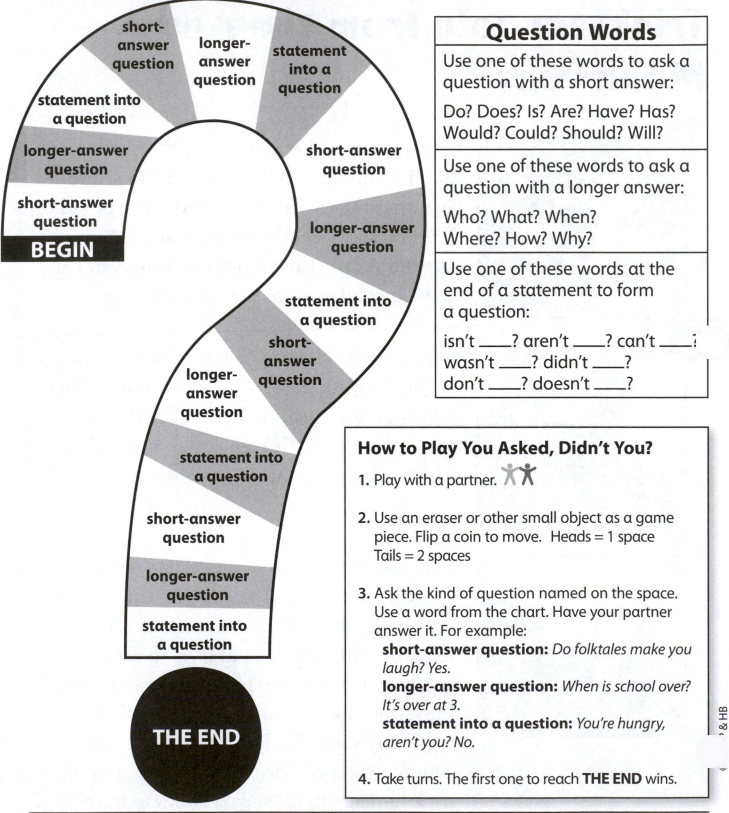

BEGIN

short-answer question

longer-answer question

statement into a question

short-answer question

longer-answer question

statement into a question

short-answer question

longer-answer question

statement into a question

short-answer question

longer-answer question

statement into a question

short-answer question

longer-answer question

statement into a question

short-answer question

longer-answer question

THE END

Question Words

Use one of these words to ask a question with a short answer:

Do? Does? Is? Are? Have? Has? Would? Could? Should? Will?

Use one of these words to ask a question with a longer answer:

Who? What? When? Where? How? Why?

Use one of these words at the end of a statement to form a question:

isn't ____? aren't ____? can't ____? wasn't ____? didn't ____? don't ____? doesn't ____?

How to Play You Asked, Didn't You?

1. Play with a partner. 🧍🧍

2. Use an eraser or other small object as a game piece. Flip a coin to move. Heads = 1 space Tails = 2 spaces

3. Ask the kind of question named on the space. Use a word from the chart. Have your partner answer it. For example:
   short-answer question: *Do folktales make you laugh? Yes.*
   longer-answer question: *When is school over? It's over at 3.*
   statement into a question: *You're hungry, aren't you? No.*

4. Take turns. The first one to reach **THE END** wins.

Love and Roast Chicken

Fill in what the character says and does. Write what this shows about the character.

Character Chart

Character	What the Character Does	What the Character Says	What It Shows
Cuy			
Tío Antonio			
the farmer			

Use your character chart to retell the story to a partner.

Fluency: Expression

Love and Roast Chicken

Expression in reading is how you use your voice to express feeling. Use this passage to practice reading with proper expression.

"*¡Qué tramposo!* What a rascal! You're not a farmworker,   9

you're a guinea pig!" cried the farmer. "And you've been eating   20

all my alfalfa! Well, Florinda loves to eat roast guinea pig,   31

and tomorrow we will eat YOU!"   37

He pulled Cuy free from the sticky gum doll. Then he tied him   50

to the eucalyptus tree and went back to bed.   59

"It can't get any worse than this!" thought Cuy. But here came   71

Tío Antonio sneaking toward the chicken coop.   78

From "Love and Roast Chicken," page 90

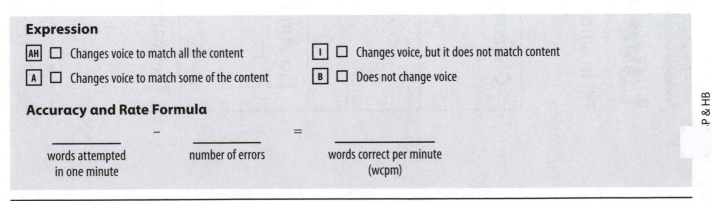

Expression

AH ☐ Changes voice to match all the content   I ☐ Changes voice, but it does not match content

A ☐ Changes voice to match some of the content   B ☐ Does not change voice

Accuracy and Rate Formula

_____ − _____ = _____

words attempted   number of errors   words correct per minute
in one minute   (wcpm)

.P & HB

Name _____ Date _____

Respond and Extend: Venn Diagram

Compare Characters' Adventures

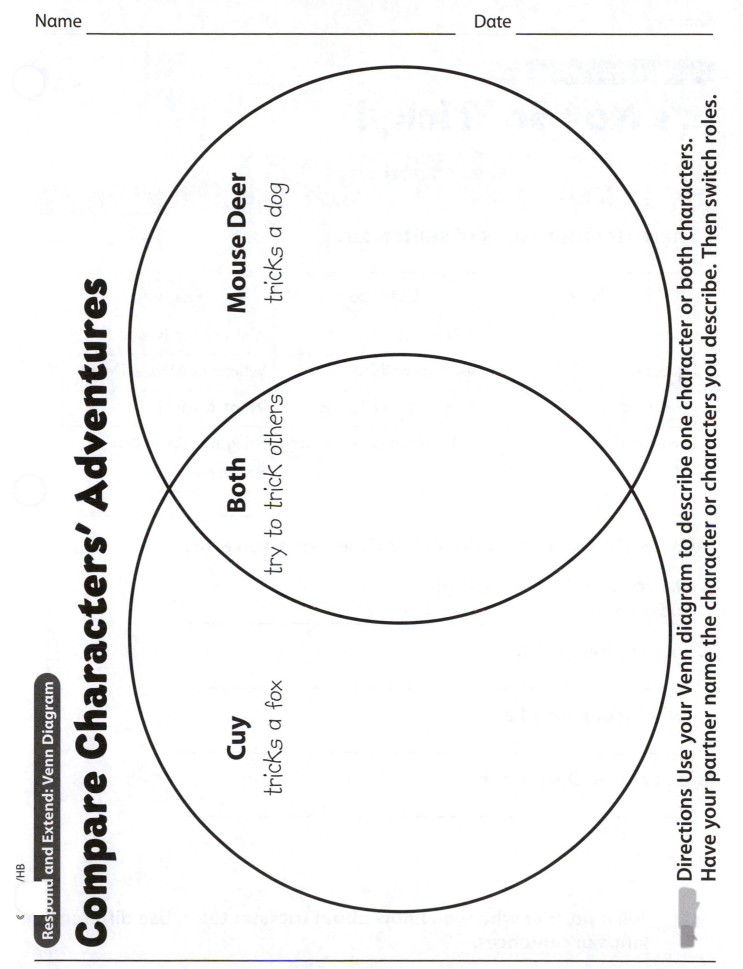

Cuy
tricks a fox

Both
try to trick others

Mouse Deer
tricks a dog

Directions Use your Venn diagram to describe one character or both characters.
Have your partner name the character or characters you describe. Then switch roles.

Grammar: Kinds of Sentences

It's Not So Tricky!

Grammar Rules Kinds of Sentences

There are four kinds of sentences.

Name	Definition	Example
statement	tells something	Mouse Deer is smart.
question	asks something	Where is Mouse Deer?
exclamation	shows strong feeling	What a trick!
command	tells you to do something	Bring me some food. Be careful!

Name each sentence. Then write each sentence correctly.

1. **where does Mouse Deer go**

   question Where does Mouse Deer go? _____

2. **he is in the garden**

   _____

3. **what a big mistake**

   _____

4. **tell Mouse Deer to run**

   _____

Tell a partner what you know about trickster tales. Use different kinds of sentences.

& HB

Identify Main Idea and Details

Complete a main idea diagram about the kinds of commands that dogs follow.

Main Idea: Dogs can follow many different commands.

Detail: 1.
Detail: 2.
Detail: 3.

/HB

Grammar: Combining Sentences

Cat and Mouse

Grammar Rules Combining Sentences

Compound sentences include two ideas. A connecting word joins the two ideas into one longer sentence.

Idea #1	Connecting Word	Idea #1	New Sentence	
Cats like to hunt.	and	They chase mice.	Cats like to hunt, and they chase mice.	

Join the sentences. Use *or, and,* or *but*. Remember to use a comma to separate the sentences.

1. **Our cat is very small. It hides easily.**

2. **It stalks a mouse. The mouse runs.**

3. **Mom takes the cat off the bed. It jumps back up.**

4. **The cat comes when I call. It ignores me.**

Tell a partner two ideas about an animal you know. Connect your ideas in a compound sentence.

& HB

Animal Smarts

1

Animals are smarter than we used to think. They can use tools and communicate. They show intelligence in many ways.

2

People thought animals could not use tools. A scientist discovered chimpanzees that used sticks to get termites. We know that animals imitate each other and can learn to use tools.

3

Some animals communicate with each other, or with humans. Koko the gorilla uses sign language. Meerkats communicate with each other using different sounds. Even dogs understand language!

4

Scientists learn about animals by observing their intelligence. In the future, we will know even more about how animals think.

Grammar: Complex Sentences

Why Or When?

Grammar Rules Complex Sentences

Only one part of a complex sentence can stand alone as a complete thought.

- Use a conjunction such as *when* or *because* to join the two parts.
- Choose the conjunction that expresses the right relationship.

When people talk, Koko answers.

The guard yelps because danger is near.

Use *when* or *because* to make a complex sentence.

1. they are young | animals already know some things

When they are young, animals already know some things.

2. animals can learn tricks | they are smart

3. she was young | Koko learned sign language

4. Koko can communicate | a scientist taught her

💬 **Tell your partner about *when* you do something and *why* you do something. Use complex sentences with the words *when* and *because*.**

Name _____ Date _____

Animal Smarts

Make a Main Idea Diagram for "Animal Smarts."

Main Idea Diagram

Main Idea: Animals are _____.
Detail:
Detail:
Detail:
Detail:
Detail:
Detail:
Detail:

Use your main idea diagram to explain the selection to a partner.

Animal Smarts

Use this passage to practice reading with proper intonation.

To play a trick on someone may take some intelligence, too.   11

You have to guess how the person will act. Then you have   23

to find a way to trick the person. Some animals have been   35

terrific tricksters.   37

An orangutan named Fu Manchu tricked the zookeepers   45

at the Omaha Zoo. He escaped from his home three times.   56

First, he traded food with another orangutan for a piece of wire.   68

Then he hid the wire in his mouth. Finally, he used the wire to   82

pick the lock and set himself free!   89

From "Animal Smarts," page 122

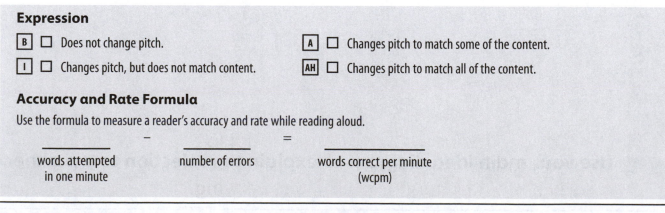

Expression

B ☐ Does not change pitch.   A ☐ Changes pitch to match some of the content.

I ☐ Changes pitch, but does not match content.   AH ☐ Changes pitch to match all of the content.

Accuracy and Rate Formula

Use the formula to measure a reader's accuracy and rate while reading aloud.

_____ − _____ = _____
words attempted   number of errors   words correct per minute
in one minute   (wcpm)

Name _____   Date _____

"The Clever Chimps of Fongoli"

What I think:	What do you think?
Page:	
Page:	
Page:	

Practice explaining your thoughts aloud. In a group of four, talk about details of the science article that you agreed or disagreed on. Each of you should explain your thinking.

HB

©

Compare Information

Directions: Put a check mark next to each fact if you find it in the article. Find more facts and write them on your chart.

Comparison Chart

Fact	Animal Smarts	The Clever Chimps of Fongoli
Chimps walk on the ground.	✓	✓
Rainforest chimps live in trees.		✓
Chimps eat insects.		
Some chimps eat bush babies.		
In 1960, Jane Goodall made an important discovery about chimps.		
Chimps use tools.		

Take turns with a partner. Ask each other questions about the information provided in the two science articles.

© & HB

Name _____   Date _____

The Game of Coordination

Grammar Rules Combining Sentences

1. Join two complete sentences with a conjunction like *and*, *or*, or *but*. Use a comma before the conjunction.

    > My dog likes to learn new tricks, but my cat just likes to sleep.

2. Join an incomplete and a complete sentence with a conjunction like *because* or *when*. Use a comma when needed.

    > Because dogs understand language, they respond to commands

Underline conjunctions. Circle commas that separate ideas.

When my cousin came to visit, we went to the aquarium.

I learned about many water animals. My cousin liked the sharks,

but I liked the octopus. When I saw the octopus go through a maze,

I knew it had a good memory. When the octopus first tried the

maze, it made mistakes. Because it learned the way, it never makes

mistakes now. Now aquarium workers are teaching her different

shapes. I like this octopus, and my cousin admitted she did, too!

Write a compound sentence and a complex sentence to add to the story. Read them to a partner.

Development of Ideas

	How thoughtful and interesting is the writing?	How well are the ideas explained and supported?
4 **Wow!**	• The writing is engaging. • It is filled with strong, interesting ideas.	• The main idea is clear. • The details are well developed.
3 **Ahh.**	• Most of the writing is engaging. • It is somewhat filled with strong, interesting ideas.	• Most of the main idea is clear. • Most of the details are well developed.
2 **Hmm.**	• Some of the writing is engaging. • There are some strong, interesting ideas.	• The main idea is not very clear. • There are a few interesting details.
1 **Huh?**	• The writing is not engaging. • It does not include interesting ideas.	• There is no main idea. • There are no details.

Main Idea Diagram

Complete the Main Idea Diagram for your business letter.

Main Idea:

Detail:

Detail:

Detail:

Name _____   Date _____

Revise

Use the Revising Marks to revise this letter.
Look for:

- information organized in a logical order
- appropriate language

Revising Marks

∧	Add.
℘	Take out.
⟳↗	Move to here.

Dear Dr. Miller!

How smart are chimps? My class has been learning about different animals and how smart they are. Would you please answer some questions for me?

Second, what commands can chimps learn? First, can chimps learn to do any simple tasks? Finally, what is the best way to train a chimp to learn something? Thank you for your help.

Bye!

Jeff Johnson

Writing Project

Edit and Proofread

Use the Editing Marks to edit and proofread this passage. Look for:

- **correct spelling of vowel sounds in words**

- **correct capitalization and punctuation of addresses**

- **correct punctuation of sentences**

Editing Marks

∧	Add.
ℒ	Take out.
⬭⌒∧	Move to here.
⌄∧	Add comma.
⊙∧	Add period.
＝	Make it a capital letter.

Dr. amir Patel

Boston University

202 Lincoln Boulevard

Boston ma 02115

Dear Dr. Patel:

I am writing becawse I have some questions for you. I want to knouw how smart elephants are. Can you help me?

First, can elephants learn simple commands? I know dogs can learn tricks. They can follow some commands. Can people teach elephants any tricks? Thank you for you help?

Sincerely,

Michelle Williams

HB

©

Name _____   Date _____

Amazing Places

Make a concept map with the answers to the Big Question:
Why learn about other places?

© & HB

Thinking Map: Theme Chart

Story Theme

Make a theme chart about a story you know.

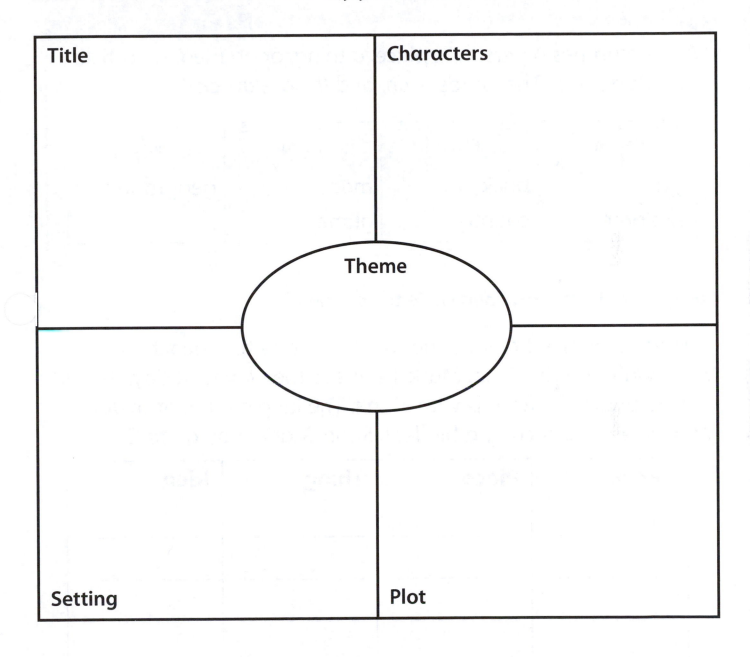

Title

Characters

Theme

Setting

Plot

💬 **Use your theme chart to tell a partner about the story.**

Name _____   Date _____

Grammar: Nouns and Articles

Kate's Treasure Map

Grammar Rules Nouns and Articles

A noun names a person, a place, a thing, or an idea. An article signals a noun. The words *a, an,* and *the* are articles.

Person	Place	Thing	Idea
girl	backyard	map	geography
explorer	country	globe	

Categorize the nouns. Then circle the articles.

Marie travels in her imagination. Marie flies to a beach in Cuba. Marie walks on the sand. Marie listens to the waves. Today, the girl visits a jungle. Tía Rosa is with Marie. The jungle is full of beauty. Marie sees an ant carry a big leaf. Soon, Marie may go to China!

Person	Place	Thing	Idea
Marie			

Where do you go in your imagination? What do you see? Tell a partner. Have your partner write down some of your nouns.

How I Learned Geography

1

A boy and his family left their country because of war. They lived in a small room. They had no toys or books, and very little food. One night, Father returned home with a map instead of bread. The boy was very angry.

2

The next day, Father hung up the map. The boy began to study the map. He traveled to faraway countries without even leaving the room.

3

The boy saw deserts, beaches, and mountains. He saw temples, fruit groves, and tall buildings. He spent many hours away from his hunger. He understood that his father was right after all.

Grammar: Plural Nouns with -s and -es

In a Box Game

Grammar Rules Plural Nouns with -s and -es

1. To make most nouns plural, just add -s.
2. If the noun ends in s, z, sh, ch, or x, add -es.
3. If the noun ends in y after a consonant, change the y to i and add -es.

1. **Play with a partner.**

2. **Choose a box without a person's initials in it. Change the noun in the box to a plural. Spell it aloud.**

3. **If your partner agrees with the plural, write your initials in the box.**

4. **When all boxes are taken, count your boxes. The player with the most boxes is the winner.**

bush	country	globe	ditch
bushes			
_____	_____	_____	_____
inhabitant	kiss	range	fox
_____	_____	_____	_____
church	bunny	penny	crash
_____	_____	_____	_____
wish	watch	buzz	berry
_____	_____	_____	_____

Reread and Summarize: Theme Chart

"How I Learned Geography"

Make a theme chart for "How I Learned Geography."

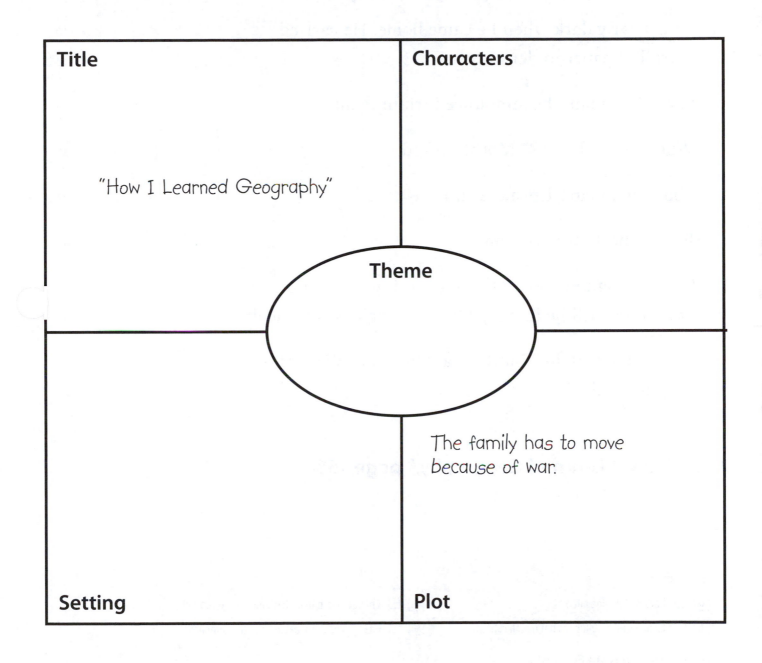

Title	Characters
"How I Learned Geography"	

Theme

Setting	Plot
	The family has to move because of war.

Use your theme chart to summarize the story and state the theme.

©/HB

"How I Learned Geography"

Use this passage to practice reading with proper intonation.

It was nearly dark when he came home. He carried	10
a long roll of paper under his arm.	18
"I bought a map," he announced triumphantly.	25
"Where is the bread?" Mother asked.	31
"I bought a map," he said again.	38
Mother and I said nothing.	43
"I had enough money to buy only a tiny piece of bread,	55
and we would still be hungry," he explained apologetically.	64
"No supper tonight," Mother said bitterly. "We'll have	72
the map instead."	75

From "How I Learned Geography," page 158

Intonation

B ☐ Does not change pitch.	A ☐ Changes pitch to match some of the content.
I ☐ Changes pitch, but does not match content.	AH ☐ Changes pitch to match all of the content.

Accuracy and Rate Formula

use the formula to measure a reader's accuracy and rate while reading aloud.

_____	−	_____	=	_____
words attempted in one minute		number of errors		words correct per minute (wcpm)

P/HB

Name _____ Date _____

Tortillas Like Africa

Complete this chart as you read "Tortillas Like Africa."

Page	Details	What I Visualize
169	We dusted the cutting board with flour.	

/HB

💬 **How do the details help you visualize what is happening?**

Respond and Extend: Figurative Language Chart

Compare Figurative Language

Write metaphors and similes you find in the story and the poem. Label each metaphor and simile.

"How I Learned Geography"	"Tortillas Like Africa"
"Our cheerless room was flooded with color." (metaphor)	Here was Chile, thin as a tie." (simile)

Take turns with a partner. Tell how each metaphor or simile helps you picture what is happening.

Grammar: Plural Nouns

Moving Day

Grammar Rules Plural Nouns

1. To make many nouns plural, add -s to the end.

   land ➝ lands

2. For nouns that end in *x, ch, sh, s, z* and sometimes *o*, add -es.

   bench ➝ benches   tomato ➝ tomatoes

3. For nouns that end in *y* after a consonant, change the *y* to *i* and add -es.
   For nouns that end with a vowel then *y*, just add -s.

   lady ➝ ladies   way ➝ ways

Write the plural nouns.

I looked around at our new home. The floor was covered

in ___*boxes*___ . My mother was unpacking _____ in the kitchen.
   (box)   (glass)

In three _____ I started school. I wondered if my _____
      (day)   (class)

would be hard. I wondered if these _____ played football. My
                          (boy)

two little _____ did not seem worried. Mama saw the look on
     (sister)

my face. She said there were other _____ from Mexico on our
                 (family)

block. She said some of the _____ were from other _____,
        (coach)   (country)

too. I started to feel better about my new home.

> **Pick two plural nouns from above and write new sentences.
> Read them to a partner.**

Thinking Map: Main Idea and Details

Logical Order

Write the main idea and two details for the last two places Ethan visits.

Outline

I. Ethan goes to London. _____

    A. _____

    B. _____

II. _____

    A. _____

    B. _____

Work with a partner. Take turns using your outline to tell about the last two places that Ethan visited.

Can You Count It?

Grammar Rules Count and Noncount Nouns

- Some nouns are things that can be counted. Their plural forms often end in *-s* or *-es*.
- Some nouns cannot be counted. They do not have a plural form.

Look at the words in the box. Write the plural form of each word in the chart below. Write the items you can count on the left side of the chart. Write the items you cannot count on the right side of the chart.

| star | snow | bush | sand | story | rock | apple |
| water | chair | ice | box | mud | rain | rice |

Can Be Counted	Cannot Be Counted
stars	snow

What pattern do you see in your chart?

_____

_____

_____

Name _____   Date _____

Extreme Earth

1

Mount Everest is the tallest mountain on Earth. It is 8,850 meters (29,035 feet) above sea level. Plants and animals do not live on the snowy, icy mountain.

2

The Sahara Desert is the world's largest desert. It only gets 3 inches of rain each year. Summer temperatures are often 90° Fahrenheit. A few plants and animals live here.

3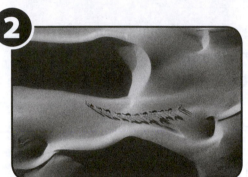

The Great Barrier Reef is the largest reef on Earth. Over time, tiny coral have formed the reef. Many marine animals live on the reef, including fish, turtles, and dolphins.

4

Angel Falls is the world's tallest waterfall. Water drops 3,212 feet. Millions of years ago, wind and water wore away a plateau. Angel Falls flows over it.

Grammar: Proper Nouns

A Proper Game

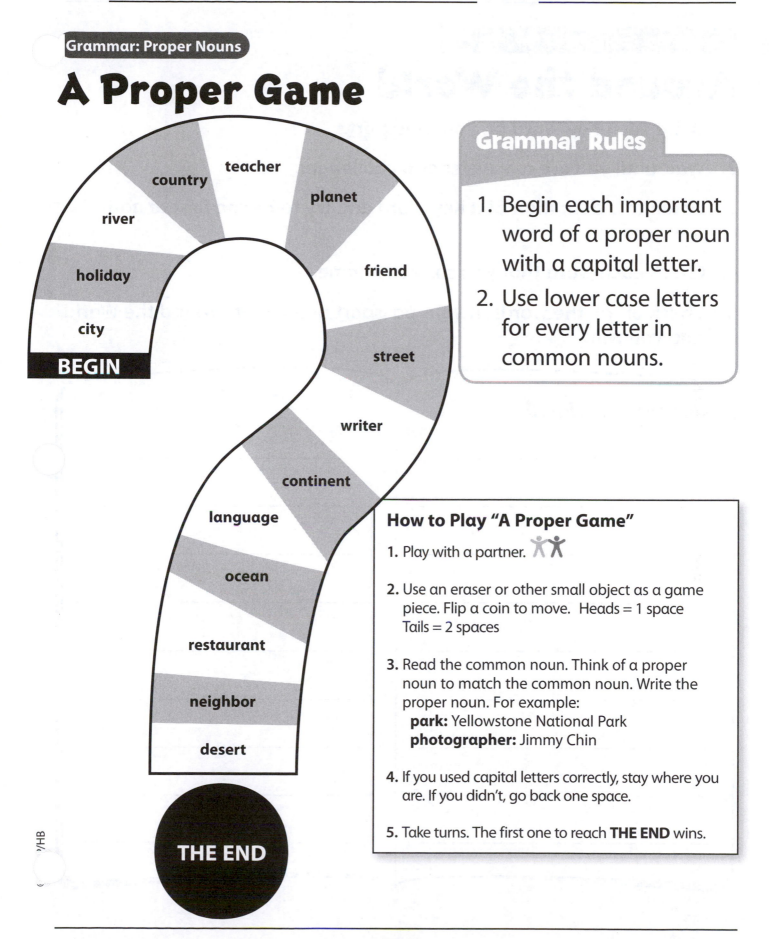

teacher
country
planet
river
friend
holiday
street
city
BEGIN
writer
continent
language
ocean
restaurant
neighbor
desert
THE END

Grammar Rules

1. Begin each important word of a proper noun with a capital letter.
2. Use lower case letters for every letter in common nouns.

How to Play "A Proper Game"

1. Play with a partner.

2. Use an eraser or other small object as a game piece. Flip a coin to move. Heads = 1 space Tails = 2 spaces

3. Read the common noun. Think of a proper noun to match the common noun. Write the proper noun. For example:
   park: Yellowstone National Park
   photographer: Jimmy Chin

4. If you used capital letters correctly, stay where you are. If you didn't, go back one space.

5. Take turns. The first one to reach **THE END** wins.

/HB

Vocabulary: Apply Word Knowledge

Around the World

1. Write each Key Word on your passport.

2. Wait until you are a traveler or a challenger.

3. Listen to a definition of a Key Word and try to be the first to name the word.

4. Check each word that you correctly name.

5. Check off all the words in your passport or make it Around the World, and you win!

Around the World

_____   _____

_____   _____

_____   _____

_____   _____

_____   _____

_____   _____

_____   _____

_____   _____

Name _____ Date _____

Outline the main ideas and details in "Extreme Earth."

Outline

    I. **Mount Everest is the tallest mountain on the planet.**

        A. **It is 8,850 meters above sea level.**

        B. **No plants or animals live there.**

    II. **The Sahara is the largest hot desert on Earth.**

        A. **Only 8 centimeters of rain fall each year.**

        B. Few plants and animals live there.

    III. _____

        A. _____

        B. _____

    IV. _____

        A. _____

        B. _____

    V. _____

        A. _____

        B. _____

    VI. _____

        A. _____

        B. _____

Use your outline to summarize "Extreme Earth" with a partner. Include Key Words in your main ideas and details.

Fluency: Phrasing

"Extreme Earth"

Use this passage to practice reading with proper phrasing.

Our next extreme place is under water. It is the Great	11
Barrier Reef, off the coast of Australia. It is the largest reef on	24
Earth. It is bigger than New Mexico. In fact, the Great Barrier	36
Reef is the largest thing ever built by living creatures.	46
The builders are tiny animals called coral polyps. Each	55
polyp takes chemicals from the sea. It uses the chemicals to	66
make a hard outer skeleton shaped like a cup. This cup	77
protects the polyp's soft body.	82

From "Extreme Earth," page 188

Phrasing

| B | ☐ Rarely pauses while reading the text. | A | ☐ Frequently pauses at appropriate points in the text. |
| I | ☐ Occasionally pauses while reading the text. | AH | ☐ Consistently pauses at all appropriate points in the text. |

Accuracy and Rate Formula
Use the formula to measure a reader's accuracy and rate while reading aloud.

$$\underline{\hspace{2cm}} \quad - \quad \underline{\hspace{2cm}} \quad = \quad \underline{\hspace{2cm}}$$

words attempted in one minute	number of errors	words correct per minute (wcpm)

"Photographing the World"

Complete this chart as you read the profile.

Page	My question	The answer

/HB

Practice asking and answering questions aloud in a group of four. One group member asks a question from the reflection journal aloud, and the next member answers it. Continue around the group until each member has asked and answered one question.

Name _____ Date _____

Photographing the World

Write yes or no next to each feature. List more text features.

features	"Extreme Earth"	"Photographing the World"
1. title	yes	yes
2. section headings		
3. photographs		
4. captions		
5. maps		

Talk about features of the two genres with a partner. Each partner can describe one of the genres. Mention all features of your genre that you listed in the chart.

& HB
©

Name _____   Date _____

Saving a Forest from Fire

Grammar Rules Irregular Plural Nouns

rule	example
Some plural nouns do not add -s or -es to show "more than one." They change their spelling.	*goose* → *geese*
Some nouns do not change at all when they become plural.	*moose* → *moose*

Write the plural form of the noun in the box to complete each sentence.

1. ⬜ deep   There are many __*deer*__ living in the forest. A fire put them in danger.

2. ⬜ fireman   It took forty _____ to put out the fire. They saved the animals and some very old trees.

3. ⬜ person   After the fire was out, many _____ offered to help.

4. ⬜ child   The town's _____ gathered food for the animals.

💬 **Pick two of the plural nouns from above and write new sentences. Read them aloud to a partner.**

Writing Project: Rubric

Organization

	Is the whole report organized?	**Does the writing flow?**
4 Wow!	• The writing is well-organized. It fits the writer's purpose.	• The writing is very smooth. Each idea flows into the next one.
3 Ahh.	• The writing is organized. It fits the writer's purpose.	• The writing is pretty smooth. There are only a few places where it jumps around.
2 Hmm.	• The writing is organized, but it doesn't fit the writer's purpose.	• The writing jumps from one idea to another idea, but I can still follow it a little.
1 Huh?	• The writing is not organized. Maybe the writer forgot to use an outline to plan.	• I can't tell what the writer wants to say.

Name _____   Date _____

Brainstorm Your Topic

Use this chart to brainstorm possible topics for your research report.
After you complete it, circle the topic that is most interesting to you.

Name of Place	State Where It Is Located	Why It Is Extreme

Name _____   Date _____

Revise

Use the Revising Marks to revise these paragraphs. Read carefully to be certain the paragraphs:

- include only details that are related
- are written in the writer's own words

Revising Marks

∧	Add.
℘	Take out.
⌒⟋	Move to here.

Carlsbad Caverns Bat Caves
by
Salina Salazar

The bat caves of Carlsbad Caverns are crawling with bats! This area is in southwestern New Mexico.

There are huge numbers of bats living in the caves. About 400,000 of them fly out of the cave at night. There are seasonal fluctuations of the numbers, as well as daily fluctuations. "Fluctuations" means changes. Sights of the stars twinkling in the sky at night can be really beautiful. The bats search for food. Then they return to the caves.

Writing Project

Edit and Proofread

Use the Editing Marks to edit and proofread the paragraph and source list. Look for:

- plural nouns with the correct spelling
- punctuation and capitalization in a source list

Editing Marks

⊙	Add period
≡	Capitalize
——	Underline

The researchers packed their boxs as they headed for the Arctic. The womans and mans who were part of the research teames were devoting their lifes to their research for a full year.

Source List

"The Arctic " World Book Encyclopedia. 2010 print

Wilderness National park service, 15 Aug 2009. web <http://www. nps.gov>

Ghei, Irma Arctic wilderness and wildlife. new york: Lake publishing Company, 2011

Power of Nature

**Make a concept map with the answers to the Big Question:
How do we relate to nature?**

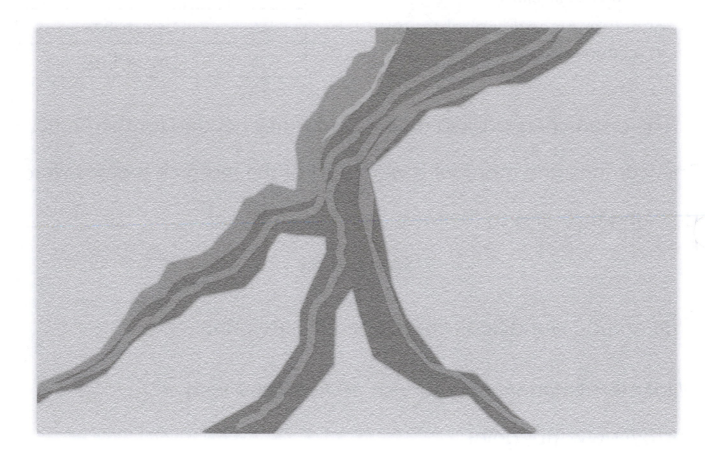

Name _____   Date _____

What Happens to Soil?

Make a cause-and-effect chart to tell what can happen to soil and why.

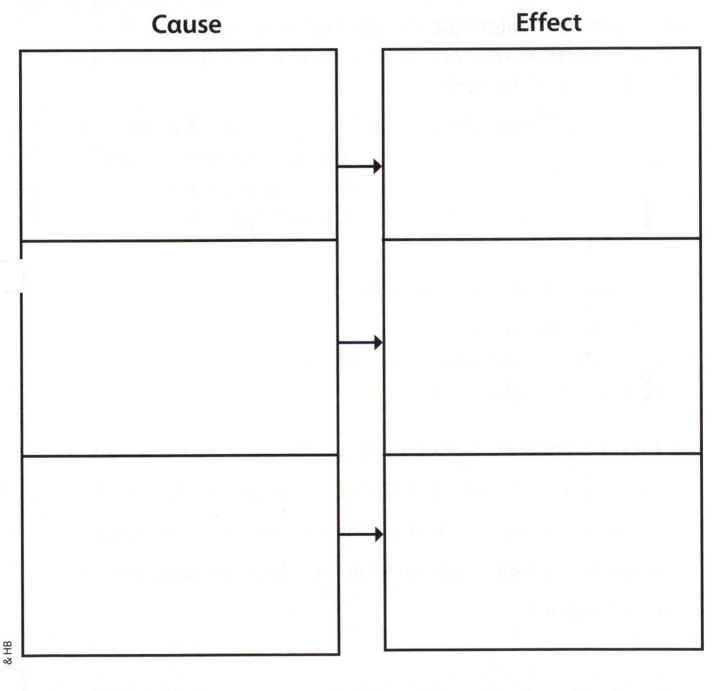

Cause   Effect

Tell a partner a cause-and-effect relationship. Use signal words such as *because*, *since*, *so*, and *as a result*.

&HB

Grammar: Present-Tense Action Verbs

Ready, Set, Go!

Grammar Rules Present-Tense Action Verb

An action verb tells what someone or something does. If the action verb tells what one other person or one thing does, use *-s* at the end of the verb.

Verb	Example Sentence
warm	The sun **warms** the land.
rush	The wind **rushes** in.
fly	A bird **flies** away.

Circle the correct present tense verb.

1. Chloe (pull/pulls) weeds.

2. The rain water (flow/flows) along the slope.

3. The soil (wash/washes) away.

Edit the paragraph. Fix four mistakes. The first one is done for you.

         looks
Chloe ~~look~~ around the store. She needs soil. She see loam and

bone meal. She is not sure which one she needs. A worker help her.

He tells her that she needs the loam. So Chloe carry loam to the

check-out stand.

Have partners talk about what a family member does when he or she gets home. Use present-tense action verbs.

Name _____ Date _____

Wind at Work

1

Wind is air that is moving. As air warms, it begins to rise. Cool air rushes in underneath. That rushing air is wind. The wind is always blowing somewhere on Earth because the planet heats and cools at different rates.

2

People use the wind to make electricity. When the wind blows, it turns turbines. They spin a generator, and the generator produces electricity. Wind is a clean, renewable resource.

3

Wind isn't always helpful. A tornado is a vertical column of spinning air. A tornado's violent wind can cause a lot of destruction. A hurricane is a huge mass of spinning clouds and wind. When a hurricane reaches land, it can cause severe damage.

© HB

Grammar: Present Progressive

What Is Happening Now?

1. Play with a partner.

2. Spin the spinner.

3. Change each sentence to make it present progressive.

For example: *I am writing to my friend about our hurricane.*

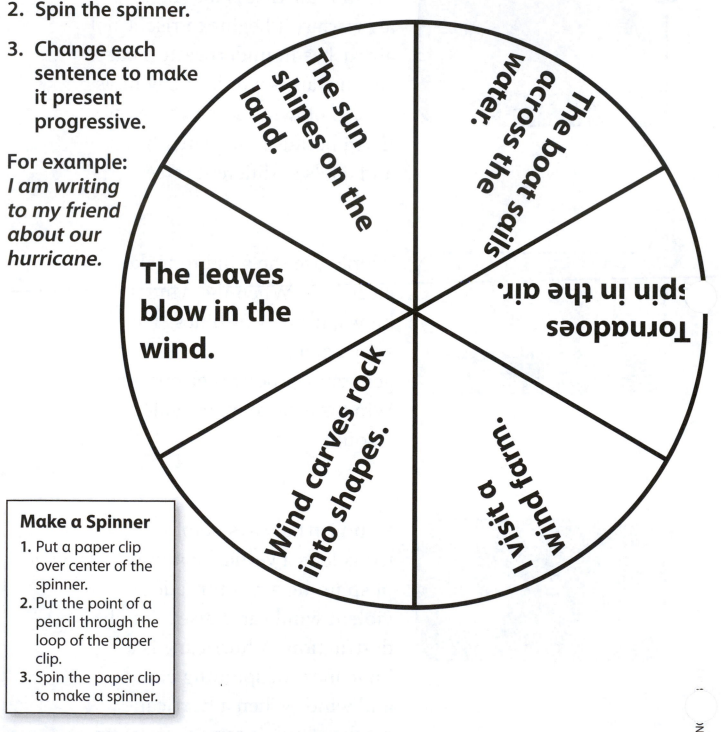

The sun shines on the land.

The boat sails across the water.

Tornadoes spin in the air.

The leaves blow in the wind.

Wind carves rock into shapes.

I visit a wind farm.

Make a Spinner

1. Put a paper clip over center of the spinner.
2. Put the point of a pencil through the loop of the paper clip.
3. Spin the paper clip to make a spinner.

Vocabulary Bingo

1. Write one Key Word in each kite.

2. Listen to the clues. Find the Key Word and use a marker to cover it.

3. Say "Bingo" when you have four markers in a row.

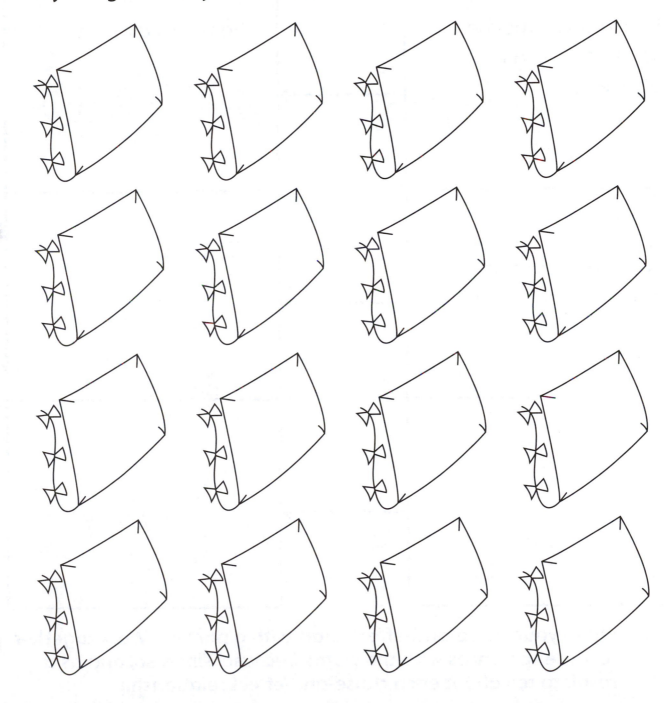

Name _____   Date _____

Wind at Work

Make a cause-and-effect chart for "Wind at Work."

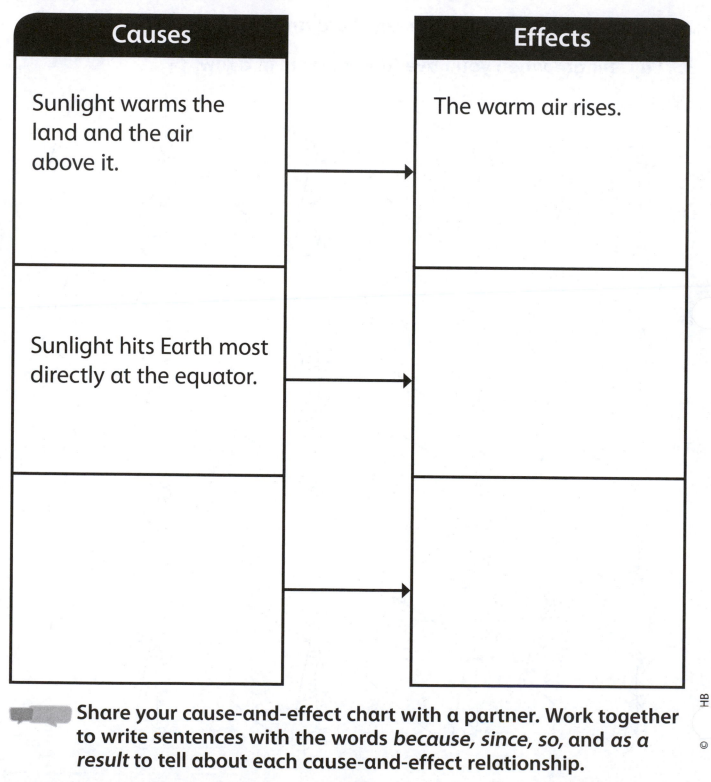

Causes	Effects
Sunlight warms the land and the air above it.	The warm air rises.
Sunlight hits Earth most directly at the equator.	

💬 **Share your cause-and-effect chart with a partner. Work together to write sentences with the words *because*, *since*, *so*, and *as a result* to tell about each cause-and-effect relationship.**

HB
©

Fluency: Intonation

Wind at Work

Use this passage to practice reading with proper intonation.

Tornadoes may be terrifying, but hurricanes are huge and	9
terrifying. A hurricane can easily stretch across three states	18
with winds that pack a major punch.	25
Hurricanes form over tropical oceans. Warm, moist air rises.	34
More air moves in underneath and then rises. Big, wet clouds	45
start to gather.	48
Over a few days, Earth's rotation causes the growing mass	58
of clouds to spin. When winds reach 119 kilometers (74 miles)	69
an hour, the storm becomes a hurricane.	76
Once hurricanes hit land, they can do extreme damage.	85
The winds can destroy trees and buildings, and huge waves	95
flood coasts.	97

From "Wind at Work," page 234

Intonation

B	☐ Does not change pitch.	A	☐ Changes pitch to match some of the content.
I	☐ Changes pitch, but does not match content.	AH	☐ Changes pitch to match all of the content.

Accuracy and Rate Formula

Use the formula to measure a reader's accuracy and rate while reading aloud.

_____	−	_____	=	_____
words attempted in one minute		number of errors		words correct per minute (wcpm)

P & HB

Name _____   Date _____

Water: The Blue Gold

Complete this chart as you read "Water: The Blue Gold."

Page	My question	The answer

💬 **Share your questions with a partner. Then reread together to find the answers.**

Name _____ Date _____

Compare Genres

Compare a science article and a persuasive essay.

	"Wind at Work"	"Water: The Blue Gold"
Topic	wind	water
Point of view: first person or third person?	third person	
Author's Purpose		
What statements from the text support the purpose?		
Does the author express a strong opinion about the topic? Give an example. Explain it.		
What did you learn?		

Take turns with a partner. Name other ways the selections are similar and different.

Lots of Action

Grammar Rules Present-Tense Action Verbs

1. An action verb tells what the subject does.
2. The verb must agree with the subject.

he, she, it, or Singular Noun: Add *-s* or *-es* to the verb.	*I, you, we, they, or Plural Noun:* Add nothing to the verb.
Mom **tells** me to close the window.	I **listen to** the wind.
The rain **begins** to fall.	The leaves **blow** across the street.
The thunder **crashes** and **booms**.	The tree branches **bend**.

Think about a storm you have seen. Use present-tense action verbs to tell what you, other people, and things do in the storm. Write your sentences. For example: When we hear thunder, Mom turns off the TV.

_____

_____

_____

_____

_____

_____

Read your sentences to a partner.

Water: Blue Gold

Complete the persuasive chart to show the author's opinions and any supporting facts.

Supporting Fact			
Supporting Fact			
Supporting Fact			
Persuasive Opinion	We must stop polluting our water systems.		

💬 Discuss the chart with your partner. Then share your ideas with the class.

/HB
©

Problem and Solution

Make a problem-and-solution chart to tell about a problem that you solved.

Problem-and-Solution Chart

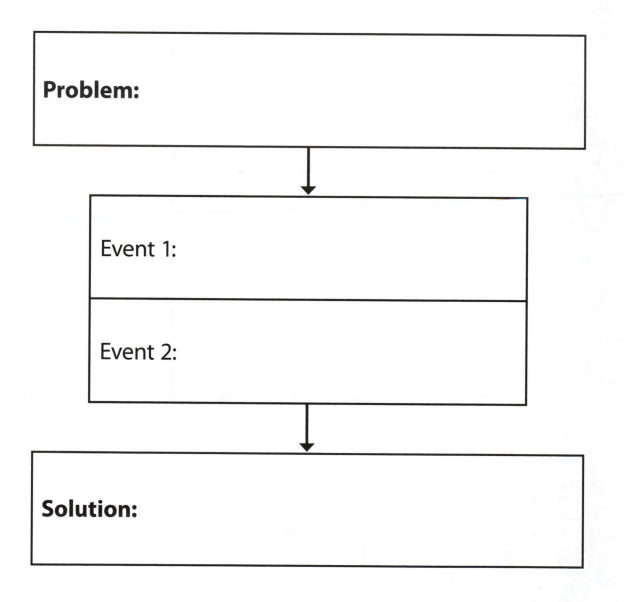

Problem:

Event 1:

Event 2:

Solution:

Share your chart with a partner. Use the chart to tell how you solved your problem.

/HB

Grammar: Forms of be

At the Beach

Grammar Rules Forms of *be*

The verbs *am, is,* and *are* link the subject of a sentence to a word in the predicate.

1. Use *am* with the subject *I*.
Use *is* to tell about one thing, one place, or one other person.
Use *are* with the subject *you* or to tell about more than one person or thing.

2. You can use a contraction to write a short form of the subject and verb.

We are surfers.	We're surfers.
It is huge!	It's huge!

Write *am, is,* or *are* to complete each sentence. Then write a contraction for the subject and verb.

1. I ___am/I'm___ happy.

2. It _____ a sunny day.

3. He _____ a great surfer.

4. I _____ a good surfer, too.

5. We _____ both happy surfers.

Tell a partner about an outdoor place you enjoy. Use *am, is,* and *are* in sentences to tell about the place.

Grammar: Forms of *be*

At the Park

Grammar Rules **Present Progressive**

Use *am*, *is*, and *are* with an *–ing* verb to tell about an action as it is happening.

Use *am* before the *-ing* verb if the subject is *I*.	I *am going* to the park.
Use *is* before the *-ing* verb if the subject is *he, she, it*, or a singular noun.	My friend *is walking* there now.
Use *are* before the *-ing* verb if the subject is *we, you, they*, or a plural noun.	We *are hoping* to have fun.

Use *am*, *is*, or *are* before the *-ing* form of the verb below. Make sure that the helping verb *am*, *is*, or *are* agrees with the subject.

I __am__ enjoying my day at the park. We _____ having fun.

Ramón _____ riding his skateboard. Sofia and Nuria _____

putting on their skates. They _____ all wearing helmets.

Dwayne _____ pushing his little sisters on the swings. They

_____ laughing. I _____ having a great time.

Which subjects and verbs can be combined above to form contractions? Turn and talk with a partner to find them.

Name _____ Date _____

Doña Flor

1

When Doña Flor was a baby, her mother sang to her, and Flor grew and grew. She knew the languages of many animals. She used her giant size to help her friends and neighbors.

2

One day, her neighbors told her they were scared of a giant mountain lion roaring very loudly. Doña Flor looked for it, but she couldn't find it.

3

Doña Flor's animal friends told her to look on the mesa. She found a little puma roaring into a hollow log. He growled at Doña Flor, but without the log, he wasn't very fierce.

4

Her neighbors came to the mesa to find Doña Flor, even though they were scared. She introduced them to her new friend. Then she lit their way home with a star and made a bed of clouds so she could rest.

© HB

Grammar: Forms of *have* and Helping Verbs

Imagine This!

Grammar Rules Forms of *have* and Helping Verbs

Use *have* or *has* to tell what belongs to someone or something.	The farm *has* windmills.
Use *can* to tell what someone or something is able to do.	A wood fire *can warm* your home.
Use *could, may,* or *might* to tell what is possible.	The storm *might blow* down trees.
Use *should* to express an opinion.	We *should use* solar energy.

1. **Play in groups of 3 to 5. One student is the referee. The others are players.**

2. **Each group chooses 10 or more Language Builder Picture Cards from any unit. Cards may show people, animals, objects, or scenes.**

3. **Taking turns, each player draws a card from the deck and tells about it, using a verb from the chart.**

4. **If the player uses the verb correctly, he or she keeps the card. If not, the card goes back into the deck. The referee decides.**

5. **Continue playing until all of the cards are used. If you wish, shuffle the deck and play again!**

The children have kites.

The kites may fly away.

Vocabulary: Apply Word Knowledge

Word Race

1. **Play with a partner.**

2. **Write one Key Word on each game board space.**

3. **Flip a coin. Move 1 space for heads. Move 2 spaces for tails.**

4. **Read the word. Tell what it means and use it in a sentence.**

5. **The first player to reach the finish wins.**

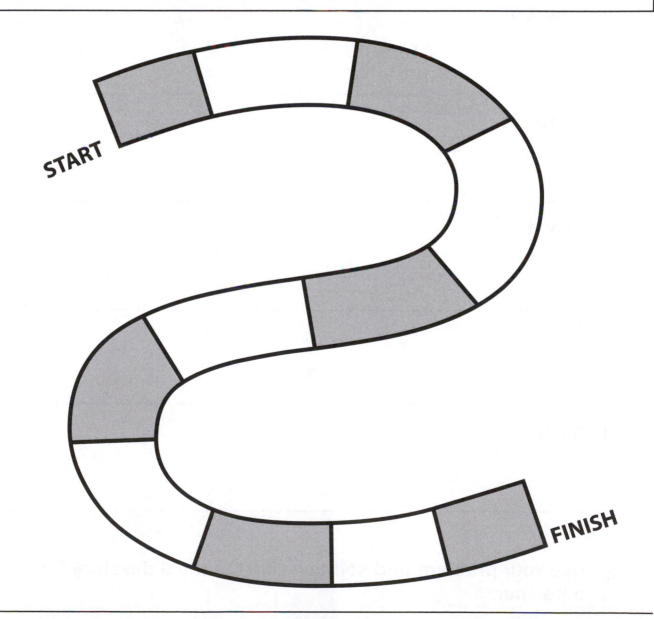

Doña Flor

Complete a problem-and-solution chart to retell the story of "Doña Flor."

Problem: Puma frightens Doña Flor's friends.

↓

Event 1:
Event 2:
Event 3:

↓

Solution:

💬 **Use your problem-and-solution chart to retell the story for a partner.**

"Doña Flor"

Use this passage to practice reading with proper expression.

Doña Flor just smiled at that brave cat and said, "Why, you're 12

just a kitten to me, Pumito." She bent down and scratched that 24

puma behind the ears, and she whispered to him in cat talk 36

until that cat began to purr. 42

Suddenly Flor heard a new noise. "Doña Flor, ¿dónde estás? 52

Where are you?" called her worried neighbors. Even though they 62

were frightened, they had all come, holding hands, looking for her. 73

"Meet my new amigo," said Doña Flor. 80

That evening, Flor plucked a star and plunked it on the tallest 92

tree so her friends in the pueblo could find their way home. 104

From "Doña Flor," page 264

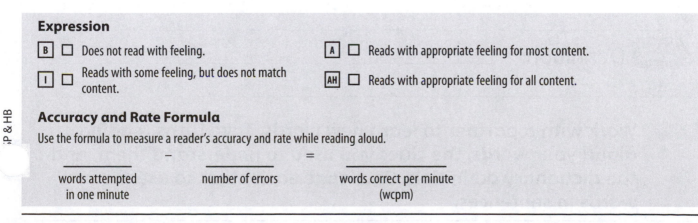

Expression

B ☐ Does not read with feeling.

I ☐ Reads with some feeling, but does not match content.

A ☐ Reads with appropriate feeling for most content.

AH ☐ Reads with appropriate feeling for all content.

Accuracy and Rate Formula

Use the formula to measure a reader's accuracy and rate while reading aloud.

_____ − _____ = _____
words attempted   number of errors   words correct per minute
in one minute   (wcpm)

"Comida"

Write down a word you don't know from each poem. Write what you think it means and your clues. Then look up the word in the dictionary.

📖 Word Detective 📖

New Word: _____

What I think it means: _____

🔍 Clues: _____

_____

📖 Definition: _____

_____

"The Sun in Me"

📖 Word Detective 📖

New Word: _____

What I think it means: _____

🔍 Clues: _____

_____

📖 Definition: _____

_____

💬 Work with a partner to learn new words. Take turns reading aloud your words, the clues you used to understand them, and the dictionary definition. Challenge each other to use the new words in sentences.

Compare Figurative Language

Write examples of figurative language from the story and poems. Explain what they mean.

Title	Example	What It Means	What You Picture
"Doña Flor"	"the houses smelled corn good"	The houses smelled like corn, which smells good.	I picture a kitchen with people eating.
"Comida"			
"The Sun in Me"			

Compare charts with a partner. Discuss the examples of figurative language you found and compare what you think they mean.

/HB

Grammar: Forms of *be* and *have*

The Moon Is...

Grammar Rules Forms of *be* and *have*

The verbs *be* and *have* must agree with the subject.

	be	have
• Use for *I*:	am	have
• Use for *you, we,* or *they* and plural subjects:	are	have
• Use for *he, she,* or *it* and singular subjects:	is	has

Complete the sentences with forms of the verbs *to be* or *to have*. Use contractions if a subject is missing.

"The moon ___is___ Swiss Cheese," I said. "_____ serious! It _____ holes all over it."

"_____ silly," said my sister. "The holes _____ craters. They look like holes but _____ not. We _____ a book about the moon. _____ in the house."

"Well, get it quickly. Hungry mice _____ on the moon," I said. "Look, _____ eaten almost all of it."

🗨 **Read a partner part of the tall tale you are writing. Talk about how you used forms of *be* and *have*. Fix any forms that may be incorrect.**

Writing Project: Rubric

Voice and Style

	Does the writing sound real and unique?	Is the writing interesting and appropriate?
4 **Wow!**	• The writing shows who the writer is. • The writer seems to be talking right to me.	• All the words fit the purpose and audience. • The words create clear images.
3 **Ahh.**	• The writing mostly shows who the writer is. • The writer seems to care about the ideas in the writing.	• Most of the words fit the purpose and audience. • The words create some clear images.
2 **Hmm.**	• It's hard to tell who the writer is. • The writer doesn't seem to be talking to me.	• Some of the words fit the purpose and audience. • The words do not create clear images.
1 **Huh?**	• I can't tell who the writer is. • The writer doesn't seem to care.	• The words do not fit the purpose and audience. • It is hard to picture what the writer is describing.

HB

©

Writing Project: Prewrite

Problem-and-Solution Chart

Complete the problem-and-solution chart for your tall tale.

Problem:
Event 1:
Event 2:
Event 3:
Solution:

© & HB

Name ______________________ Date ______________

Writing Project

Revise

Use the Revising Marks to revise this passage. Look for:

- **vivid words**
- **details about the events**
- **actions and words that fit the character**

Revising Marks	
^	Add.
	Take out.
	Move to here.

Hakeem Handles a Lightning Bolt

Hakeem was a very big person. He had done many things to help the people in Silver City. He would have a new challenge today.

Cars and buses were moving on the highway. Hakeem looked up. He saw lightning. Then he heard a loud noise. He said, "I'm going to assist."

Hakeem saw a lightning bolt heading straight for the highway. He jumped into action. He stopped the lightning bolt.

Everyone in Silver City cheered Hakeem. "However shall we be able to show you our strong appreciation for your deeds?" one person asked. "I think that you are oh-so-brave!" Hakeem felt happy.

Edit and Proofread

Use the Editing Marks to edit and proofread this passage. Look for:

- **spelling of contractions**
- **capitalization of proper nouns**
- **subject-verb agreement**

Editing Marks

∧	Add.
℘	Take out.
⬯	Check spelling.
≡	Capitalize.

Surfer suki live in miami. She are a great athlete. She hear a loud noise and looks up. A tremendous wave is racing toward the shore. Its big enough to wash away the entire town. Children and adults is pointing and screaming.

"Ill save the town!" shouts Suki.

Suki have a giant surfboard. She grab it and holds it like a bat. She lifts the surfboard and swing it fast and hard. She knocks the giant wave back into the ocean.

Suki's friends let out a sigh of relief. Then they exclaim, "You and your surfboard is our heroes!"

& HB

©

Name _____   Date _____

Invaders!

**Make a concept map with the answers to the Big Question:
When do harmless things become harmful?**

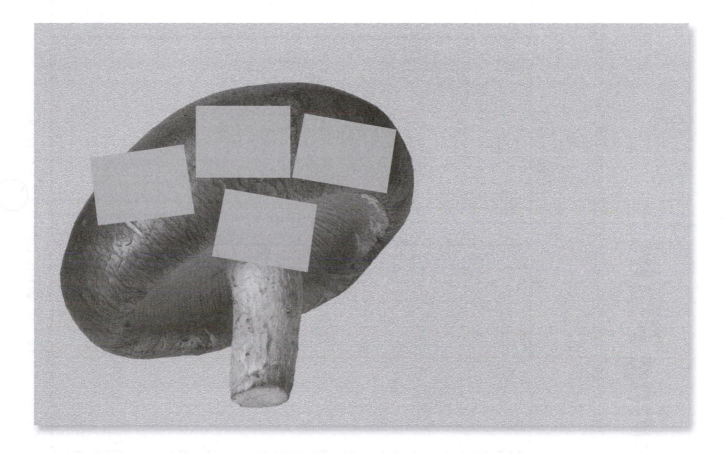

© & HB

Name _____ Date _____

A Fast Growing Plant

Complete the events chain to tell about your partner's fast growing plant.

Events Chain

```
┌─────────────────────────────────┐
│                                 │
└─────────────────────────────────┘
              ↑
┌─────────────────────────────────┐
│                                 │
└─────────────────────────────────┘
              ↑
┌─────────────────────────────────┐
│                                 │
└─────────────────────────────────┘
              ↑
┌─────────────────────────────────┐
│                                 │
└─────────────────────────────────┘
```

Use your Events Chain to retell your partner's story.

HB

©

Name _____ Date _____

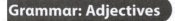
It's Nicer at the Park

Grammar Rules Adjectives

An adjective describes, or tells about, a noun.

   a **tall** tree   a **hard** rock

- Add -**er** when comparing two items.

   hard   →   hard**er**

- Add -**est** when comparing three or more items.

   tall   →   tall**est**

Write the correct adjective form.

I love going to the park. There is so much to see and do there.

There are ___ *tall* ___ trees by the swings. There are even _____
   (tall)   (tall)

trees by the pond. Someone just planted a young tree. It is the

_____ tree in the park. I like to look at the _____ flowers.
   (small)   (beautiful)

My favorites are the roses. They are the _____ flowers of all. My
                                             (pink)

brother likes to play on the swings. He can swing _____ than I
                                                       (high)

can. Sometimes my dad will get on the swings. He swings the

_____ of us all.
   (high)

HB

© ▢▢▢ **Tell a partner about a park you have seen. As you talk, have your**
         partner write down the adjectives he or she hears.

Grammar: Long Adjectives

Creepy Crawlies

Grammar Rules Long Adjectives

To compare using long adjectives, use *more* or *most* instead of *–er* or *–est*.

Use **more** to compare two people or things. Use the word *than* in the sentence.	Miki-ko is **more** talkative <u>than</u> Shelsea.
Use **most** to compare more than two people or things. Use the word *the* before the word *most*.	She is also <u>the</u> **most** fearless girl in town.

Make comparisons using *more* or *most*. Look for the words *than* or *the* to help you choose the right word. Write it on the line.

1. My friend Shelsea is ___more___ fearful than I am.

2. She calls bugs the _____ dangerous things on Earth.

3. "They are _____ distasteful than bees," I say.

4. "But they are not the _____ alarming thing on the planet."

5. "Well," she says, "You're _____ fearless than I am."

6. "But you are the _____ awesome friend!" I answer.

▰▰▰ **Turn and talk with a partner. Use adjectives to compare yourself to a friend or to someone in your family.**

HB

©

Key Points Reading

The Fungus That Ate My School

1

When the students left for vacation, they told their teacher their fungus experiments were out of control. Mr. Harrison said fungus could take care of itself.

When the students came back, fungus covered everything.

2

The fungus was in the hallways, the office, the library, the classrooms, and the cafeteria. Mr. Harrison called in a fungus expert.

3

Professor Macademia arrived to get rid of the fungus. The Fungus Unit scrubbed everything and took the fungus away. Mr. Harrison promised no more fungus experiments—until next year!

Grammar: Comparing With Adjectives

Where It Stops, Nobody Knows

Grammar Rules Comparing with Adjectives

1. An adjective can tell how many or how much.	1. The class had **many** problems.
2. The words **more** and **less** are used to compare two items.	2. The wall had **more** fungus than the floor did.
3. The words **most** and **least** are used to compare three or more items.	3. The light bulbs had the **least** mold of all.

1. Take turns in a small group.

2. Spin the spinner. Read the rule. Follow the rule to use an adjective in a sentence.

Make a Spinner

1. Put a paper clip ⌐⊃ over center of the spinner.

2. Put the point of a pencil through the loop of the paper clip ⌐⊃. Make sure the pencil goes through the paper.

3. Spin the paper clip ⌐⊃ to make a spinner.

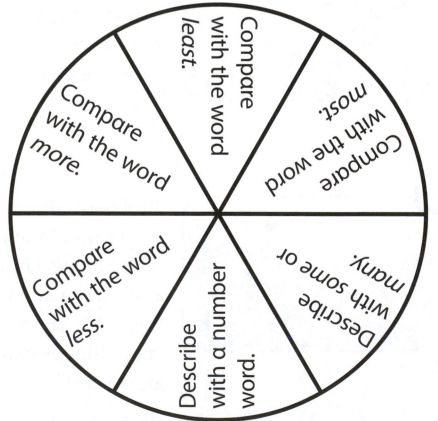

Name _____ Date _____

Reread and Retell: Events Chain

"The Fungus That Ate My School"

Make an events chain to tell what happens in "The Fungus That Ate My School."

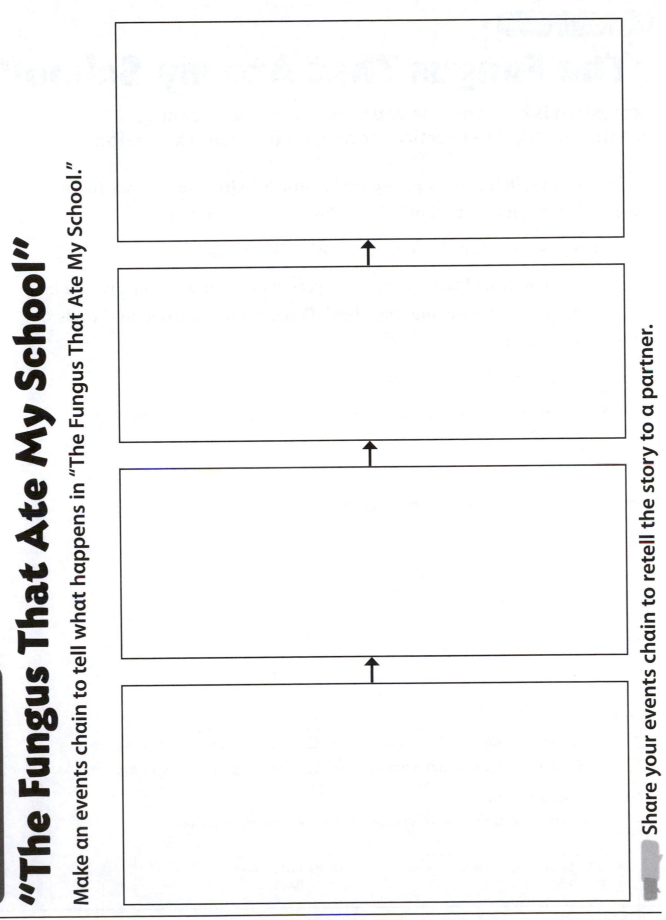

Share your events chain to retell the story to a partner.

Fluency: Expression

"The Fungus That Ate my School"

**Expression is how you use your voice to express feeling.
Use this passage to practice reading with proper expression.**

"Fresh air, light, elbow grease, and a little help from my friends in the — 14
Fungus Unit ought to get rid of IT," said Professor Macademia. — 25

"Fungus Unit? What's a Fungus Unit?" Ellen asked. — 33

"Special branch of the Sanitation Department," said someone dressed in — 43
white, pulling a giant hose into the school. Other workers carried in shovels, — 56
mops, and big lights. — 60

"Action!" called one of them. — 65

Suddenly the whole school was filled with whirring and clanking, — 75
swooshing and scrubbing. — 78

From "The Fungus that Ate My School," page 298

Expression

B ☐ Does not read with feeling.   A ☐ Reads with appropriate feeling for most content.

I ☐ Reads with some feeling, but does not match content.   AH ☐ Reads with appropriate feeling for all content.

Accuracy and Rate Formula

Use the formula to measure a reader's accuracy and rate while reading aloud.

_____ − _____ = _____
words attempted   number of errors   words correct per minute
in one minute   (wcpm)

P/HB

Name _____ Date _____

"Mold Terrarium"

Use the fact notes to write down interesting facts you learn while reading.

Amazing Facts

An amazing fact about _____

is _____

I found it in the selection _____

_____ _____
Name   Date

Amazing Facts

An amazing fact about _____

is _____

I found it in the selection _____

_____ _____
Name   Date

Amazing Facts

An amazing fact about _____

is _____

I found it in the selection _____

_____ _____
Name   Date

Work with a partner to share your facts. Take turns reading aloud your facts.

& HB

Name _____   Date _____

Compare Author's Purpose

Put a check mark by each purpose that fits the science fiction story or the science experiment.

Comparison Chart

Purpose of Genre	Science Fiction Story	Science Experiment
Tells about a science idea	✓	
Tests a science idea		✓
Tells how to do something		
Is mostly fun to read		
Describes events that can't really happen		

Work with a partner to identify each author's purpose. Write sentences to tell why an author writes a science fiction story and why an author writes a science experiment.

HB
©

Grammar: Adjectives

Gross or Good?

Grammar Rules Adjectives

1. Use adjectives to tell about color, size, or shape: **pink, brown, small, square**

2. Use adjectives to tell how something sounds, feels, looks, tastes, or smells: **loud, wet, slimy, salty, smoky**

3. Use adjectives to tell how something is used: **fishing pole, frying pan, sleeping bag**

4. Use adjectives to compare two things: **damper, more beautiful**

5. Use adjectives to compare more than two things: **biggest, most wonderful**

Choose an adjective from the box above to complete each sentence. Write the adjective on the line.

At night, Dad and I are crowded in our ___small___ tent. We hear the

_____ rain outside. In the morning, the sun is _____ than

the day before. But the ground is _____ than before. Gross! We

have been invaded by _____ worms! Dad takes out his _____

pole. "These worms are the _____ gift," says Dad. Now we

can catch the _____ fish of all!

💬 **Talk with a partner about a a gross plant or animal you've seen.
Use adjectives to describe and make comparisons.**

Identify Problem and Solution

Make a problem-and-solution chart about a problem in your environment.

Problem-and-Solution Chart

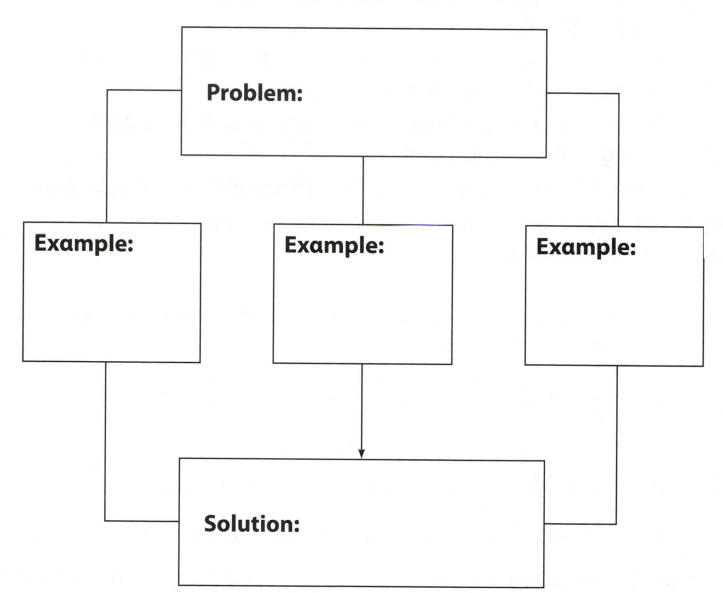

Problem:

Example:

Example:

Example:

Solution:

Share your chart with another pair of partners and see if you can come up with more solutions.

HB

©

Grammar: Possessive Adjectives

Memory Match Game

Grammar Rules Possessive Adjectives

Singular possessive adjectives show ownership by one person or thing.	Plural possessive adjectives show ownership by more than one person or thing.
my, your, her, his, its	**our, your, their**

1. Make a card for each possessive adjective below. Make two cards for the possessive adjective your, as shown.

2. Combine cards with a partner. Place all the cards facedown.

3. Take turns turning over two cards and naming the words. If the two words match, use the possessive adjective in a sentence.

4. The player with the most matches wins the game.

my	your	her	his
its	our	their	your

&HB

©

Name _____   Date _____

Aliens from Earth: When Animals and Plants Invade Other Ecosystems

1

Aliens are plants or animals that invade ecosystems. They upset an ecosystem's balance. Animals and plants have always moved around, but in the past ecosystems changed slowly.

2

Humans sped up these changes. They traveled further and faster, and they took animals and seeds. Today, it is harder to maintain the balance of earth's ecosystems.

3

Our ecosystems are no longer isolated from each other. The spread of alien species is a problem, but people can help by not carrying these species when they travel from one place to another.

Name _____ Date _____

Just Outside the Window

Grammar Rules Possessive Nouns

You can show ownership with possessive nouns.

One Owner	Add 's	the dog's tail
More Than One Owner	Add ' if the word ends in **-s** Add 's if the word does not end in **-s**	the student**s'** desks the women**'s** names

Write the possessive form of the noun on the line.

Last spring, a class found a ___robin's___ nest. Actually, they found
　　　　　　　　　　　　　　　　(robin)

two! The _____ nests were in a _____ branches. The _____
　　　　　　(birds)　　　　　　　　　　(tree)　　　　　　　　　(children)

faces were full of smiles. Ms. Ramos began a study unit on birds.

The _____ shelves were full of books on birds. Many _____
　　　　(library)　　　　　　　　　　　　　　　　　　　　　　(books)

pages explained how baby birds grew inside eggs. The children

made drawings. They put them on the _____ website. Now
　　　　　　　　　　　　　　　　　　　(school)

other _____ faces are full of smiles.
　　　　(people)

Work with a partner. Find things in the room and tell who owns them. Write a list: Gabriel's desk, the students' coats.

Name _____ Date _____

Aliens from Earth

Complete a problem-and-solution chart to tell about the main problem in "Aliens from Earth."

Problem-and-Solution Chart

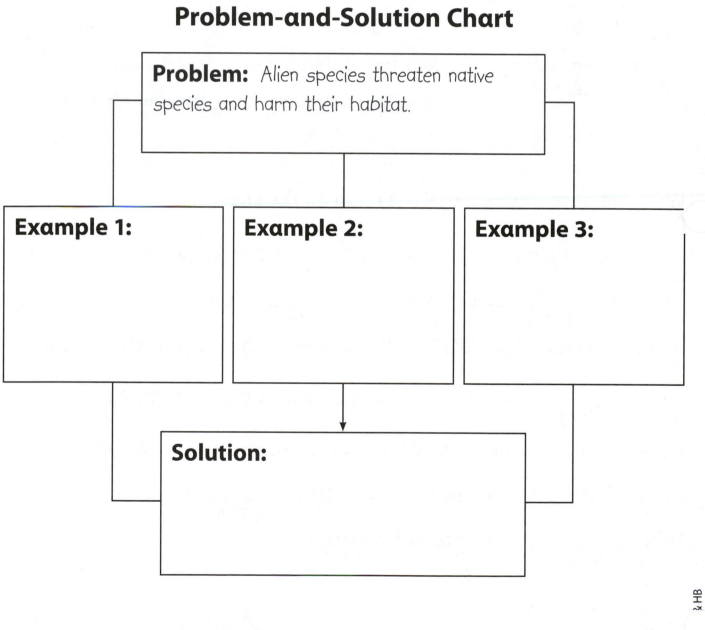

Problem: Alien species threaten native species and harm their habitat.

Example 1:

Example 2:

Example 3:

Solution:

Use your problem-and-solution chart to summarize the text for a partner.

Name _____   Date _____

"Aliens from Earth"

Use this passage to practice reading with proper phrasing.

Phrasing is how you use your voice to group words together. Punctuation marks such as periods and commas can help you group words into phrases. Use this passage to practice reading with appropriate phrasing.

Many aliens arrive in the ballast tanks of cargo ships.	10
Filled with seawater, these large tanks help ships stay	19
balanced. The tanks are like aquariums in the middle	28
of the ship. When a ship arrives in port, it empties	39
its ballast tank. This action releases thousands of	47
worms, clams, snails, and other sea creatures into an	56
ecosystem where they do not belong.	62

From "Aliens from Earth," page 330

Phrasing

B ☐ Rarely pauses while reading the text.	A ☐ Frequently pauses at appropriate points in the text.
I ☐ Occasionally pauses while reading the text.	AH ☐ Consistently pauses at all appropriate points in the text.

Accuracy and Rate Formula

Use the formula to measure a reader's accuracy and rate while reading aloud.

_____ − _____ = _____
words attempted   number of errors   words correct per minute
in one minute   (wcpm)

&HB

Name _____   Date _____

"Island Observations"

Complete the first two columns before reading. Fill in the third column as you read. Then write the questions you still have.

K-W-L-Q Chart

K What I Know	W What I Want To Know	L What I Learned	Q Questions I Still Have

💬 Tell a partner which detail was most interesting to you and why.

Name _____ Date _____

Compare Genres

Complete the Venn diagram to compare and contrast a science text and a science journal.

Venn Diagram

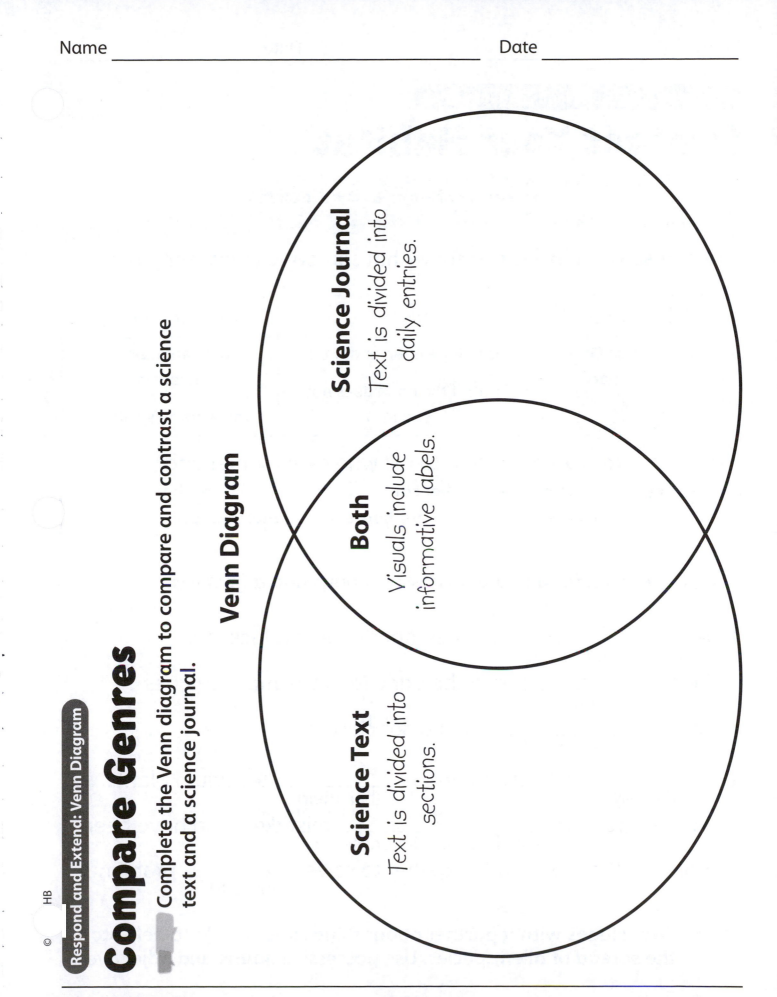

Science Journal
Text is divided into daily entries.

Both
Visuals include informative labels.

Science Text
Text is divided into sections.

Grammar: Possessive Nouns and Adjectives

Protect Your Habitat

Grammar Rules Possessive Nouns and Adjectives

Use **possessive nouns** to show that someone owns something.

One Owner	Add **'s**	a **rabbit's** hole
More Than One Owner	Add **'** if the noun ends in -**s** Add **'s** if the noun does not end in -**s**.	some **animals'** habitats the **women's** hats

Use a **possessive adjective** to tell who owns something.

my puppy   **your** mother   **her** cat   **his** hat

          its wings   **our** house   **their** skates

Write the correct form of the possessive nouns and adjectives.

1. A ___man's___ exotic pet escaped! He was lucky to
   (man's, mans')

   find _____ pet in the park. Now the man watches
          (its, his)

   the _____ behavior closely.
        (pet's, pets')

2. _____ friends dumped _____ terrarium plants
   (Me, My)   (her, their)

   in the yard. The _____ mistake could have been
                    (children's, childrens')

   harmful. We must work together to solve _____ problems.
                                            (us, our)

🗨 **Share ideas with a partner about things you can do to help stop the spread of alien species. Use possessive nouns and adjectives.**

HB ©

Name _____ Date _____

Development of Ideas

	How thoughtful and interesting is the writing?	How well are the ideas presented?
4 Wow!	• The writer has thought about the topic carefully. • The ideas are presented in a very interesting way.	• The problem and writer's opinion are very clearly stated. • The writing uses good, clear reasons and details to support the writer's opinion.
3 Ahh.	• The writer has thought about the topic. • The ideas are presented in an interesting way.	• The problem and writer's opinion are clearly stated. • The writing uses reasons and details to support the writer's opinion.
2 Hmm.	• The writer doesn't seem to have thought about the topic very much. • The writing is okay, but not interesting.	• The problem and writer's opinion are not exactly clear. • The writing uses only one or two reasons and details to support the writer's opinion.
1 Huh?	• The writer doesn't seem to have thought about the topic at all. • The ideas are presented in a boring way.	• I don't know what the problem or what the writer's opinion is. • The reasons and details don't seem related to the topic.

©/HB

Name _____ Date _____

Problem-and-Solution Chart

Complete the Problem-and-Solution Chart for your persuasive essay.

Problem-and-Solution Chart

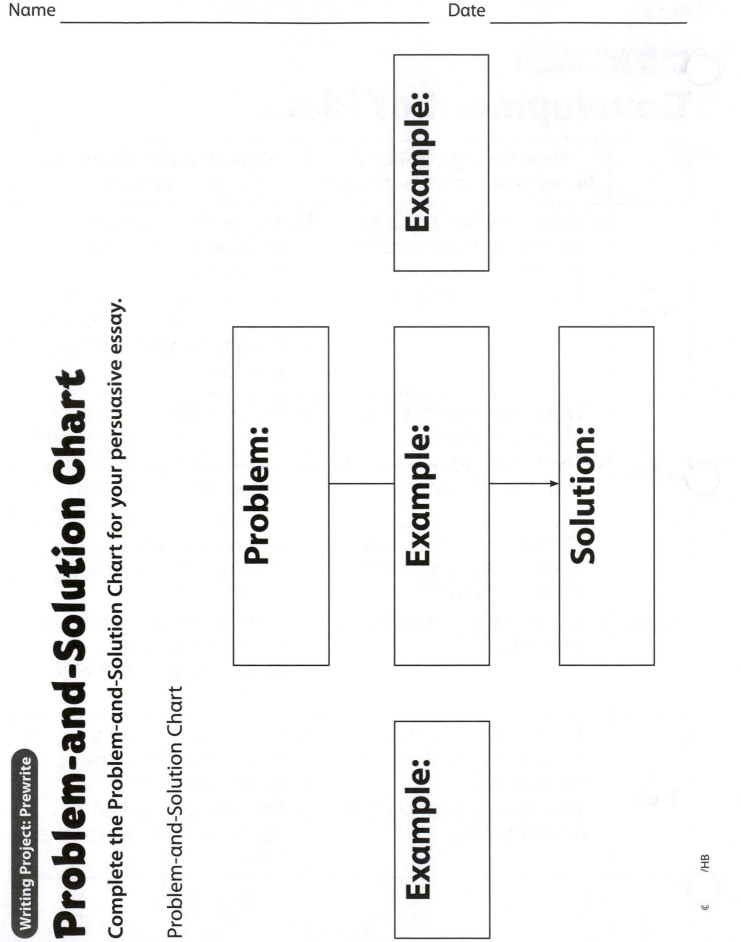

Problem:

Example:

Example:

Solution:

5.22

© /HB

Revise

Use the Revising Marks to revise this passage. Look for:

- reasons that support opinions
- persuasive language
- worthwhile ideas
- details and examples

Revising Marks

∧	Add.
℘	Take out.
⌒↗	Move to here.

Trash Trouble at the Beach

Trash on the beach creates problems. I think it is bad to throw your trash on the ground.

People make the beach dirty. They leave stuff in the sand and water. Animals can get sick. So can people who swim. Trash harms the natural habitat. It pollutes the sand and water.

If you go to the beach, do something with your trash. Put it somewhere. Consider organizing a beach clean-up day. Disposing of trash in a responsible way helps all of us.

Edit and Proofread

Use the Editing Marks to edit and proofread this passage. Look for:

- **spelling of comparative and superlative adjectives**
- **punctuation of items in a series**
- **spelling of adjectives**

Editing Marks

^	Add.
ℰ	Take out.

Water pollution is bad for people animals and plants. When people don't dispose of theires liquid waste properly, it creates problems for the environment. We need to teach our's community the responsible way to get rid of trash and other waste.

Water pollution in ours local lake means we can't swim or fish there. Chemicals in the water can kill plants and animals that live in or near the lake. An even biggerer problem comes from litter. Rain sweeps trash on the street into storm. This trash ends up in our water sources.

People must dispose of theirs chemicals and household cleaners in a responsible way. They should never pour oil paint or household cleaners down the drain. People can take these materials to the citys hazardous waste center. This is the best way to make a cleaner environment.

Name _____   Date _____

Treasure Hunters

Make a concept map with the answers to the Big Question:
Why do we seek treasure?

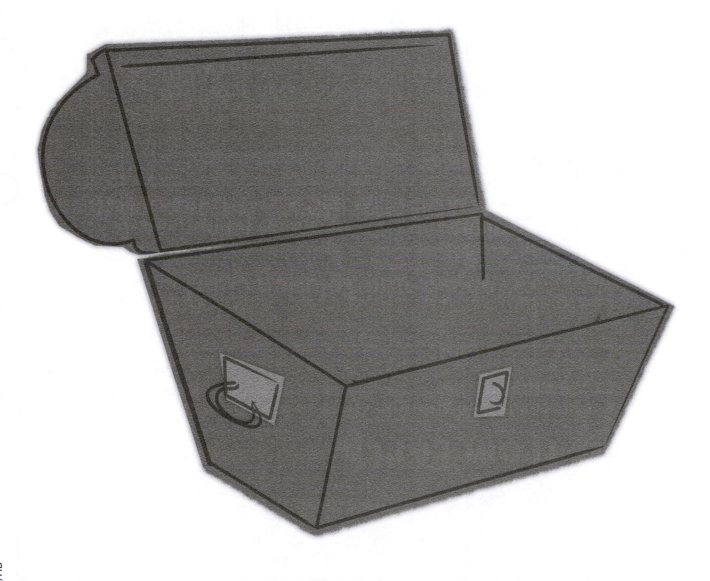

/HB

Name _____   Date _____

Finding a Treasure

Complete a character map for a favorite character. Tell how the character changes and why.

Character Map

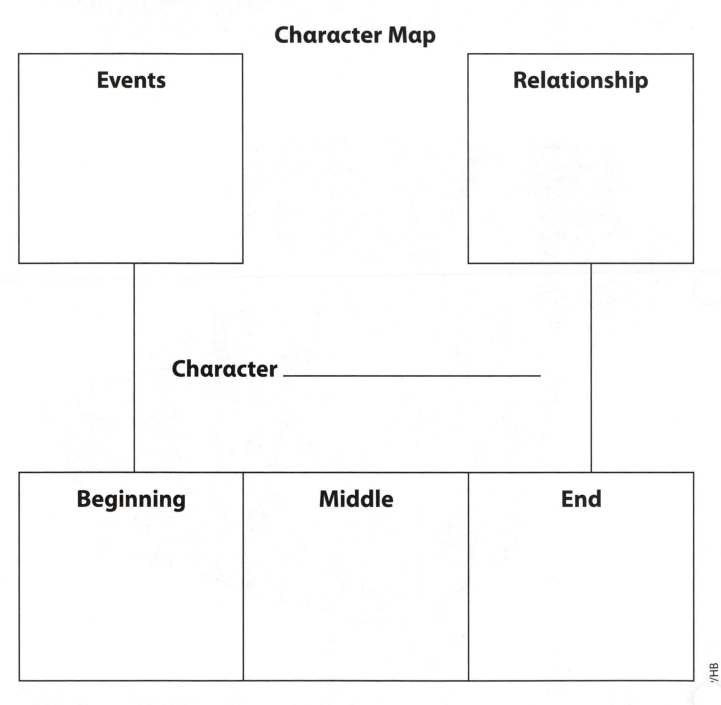

Events		Relationship

Character _____

Beginning	Middle	End

💬 **Use your Character Map to tell your partner how and why your character changed.**

Grammar: Subject and Object Pronouns

Today, We Are Pirates

Grammar Rules Subject and Object Pronouns

1. Use a subject pronoun as the subject of a sentence.
   I, you, he, she, it, we, you, they

2. Use these pronouns after a verb or after a word like *to, for, from,* or *with.*
   me, you, him, her, it, us, you, them

Read the paragraph. Replace the word or words under the line with the correct pronoun. Then partner-read the paragraph.

John and Ivan are pretending to be pirates. __*They*__ plan
(John and Ivan)

an adventure. John packs all his things. Then, _____ helps Ivan.
(John)

John packs Ivan's bag for _____ . John opens the treasure map
(Ivan)

so he can study _____ . The pirates hope to find treasure so
(the map)

_____ can be rich. Ivan's mother wishes _____ good
(the pirates)   (John and Ivan)

luck. John and Ivan wave good-bye to _____ .
(Ivan's mother)

Turn and talk in a small group. Express an intention. Use a subject or an object pronoun in your sentence, or both! Example: This spring, I plan to join our baseball team.

Name _____   Date _____

Treasure Island

1

Jim and Dr. Livesey have a map to a treasure. They hire a ship and a crew to take them to Treasure Island. They will be rich!

2

Jim hears the crew talking. They are a pirate crew and are planning to steal the ship. They want to take the treasure. Jim and Dr. Livesey plan to fight them.

3

Jim sneaks into the pirates' rowboat. On Treasure Island, he hides in a cave. He meets Ben. Ben helps Jim find Dr. Livesey.

4

The pirates attack the fort, steal the map, and capture Jim. When they dig up the treasure, there are only two gold coins!

Jim, Ben, and Dr. Livesey go back to the ship. They leave the pirates on the island.

Name _____   Date _____

Protecting Ourselves from Pirates

Grammar Rules Reflexive Pronouns

1. If you talk about a person or thing twice in a simple sentence, use a reflexive pronoun to refer back to the subject.

   Jim hid <u>himself</u> in the rowboat.

2. Make sure your reflexive pronoun ends in *-self* or *-selves*.

1. Copy the eight sentence frames onto 3 x 5 cards.

2. Combine your cards with a partner's cards. Place the cards face down.

3. Take turns turning over a card and completing the sentence with a reflexive pronoun. Read the completed sentence aloud. If your partner agrees that your sentence is correct, keep the card.

4. The player with the most cards at the end, wins the game.

Don't cut _____ with that dagger!	A rat hid _____ in the ship's hold.	The pirates told _____ that they were not bad men.	Ben hid _____ on the island.
Can we steer this ship _____?	Maria taught _____ to read a treasure map.	You boys will make _____ sick if you sail in a storm.	I opened the treasure chest all by _____.

HB ©

Treasure Island

Complete the character map to tell how Jim changes in the play.

Character Map

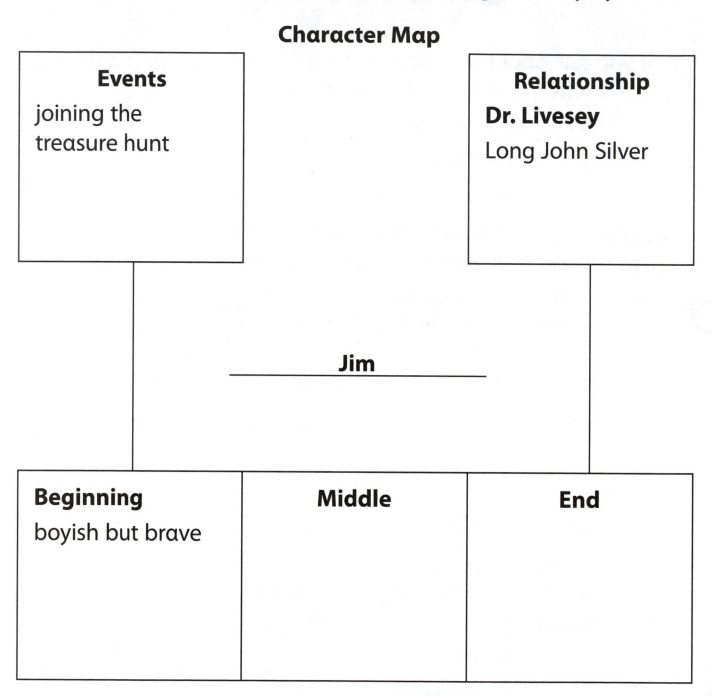

Events

joining the treasure hunt

Relationship

Dr. Livesey

Long John Silver

Jim _____

Beginning

boyish but brave

Middle

End

Use your character map to retell the story and tell how Jim changed.

HB
©

Name _____   Date _____

"Treasure Island"

Expression is how you use your voice to express feeling. Use this passage to practice reading with proper expression.

JIM [enters from offstage, alone and out of breath]: I think	11
I've lost them. [hopeless] I was foolish. Why didn't I stay with	23
my friends? [points upstage] There's a cave! I'll hide there!	33
[JIM goes into the cave. BEN GUNN enters the cave from offstage.]	45
JIM and BEN [surprised]: Oh!	50
BEN: Are you real, boy? Who are you?	58
JIM: I'm Jim Hawkins. Who are you?	65
BEN: I'm Ben Gunn. For three years I've been alone here!	76
JIM: Were you shipwrecked?	80
BEN: No, I was marooned, left here to die. I stayed alive by	93
trapping wild goats. What I wouldn't give for a bit of toasted	105
cheese! Tell me true, boy! Is that Flint's ship out there?	116

From "Treasure Island," page 373.

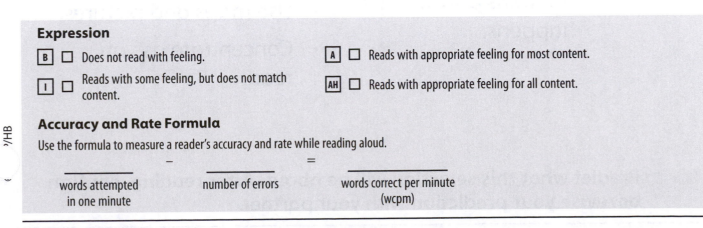

Expression

B ☐ Does not read with feeling.

I ☐ Reads with some feeling, but does not match content.

A ☐ Reads with appropriate feeling for most content.

AH ☐ Reads with appropriate feeling for all content.

Accuracy and Rate Formula

Use the formula to measure a reader's accuracy and rate while reading aloud.

_____ – _____ = _____
words attempted   number of errors   words correct per minute
in one minute   (wcpm)

>/HB

Name _____ Date _____

Make a Treasure Map

Strategy Planner

Step **1** What is the author's purpose for writing these instructions?

❏ to tell a story   **OR**   ❏ to give information

❏ to entertain

Step **2** What is your purpose for reading?

❏ for enjoyment   **OR**   ❏ for information

Step **3** What type of selection are you going to read?

❏ **fiction**   **OR**   ❏ **nonfiction**

Do the following:
- Identify the characters and settings.
- Think about what happens and when it happens.

Do the following:
- Read more slowly.
- Identify steps in a process.
- Use maps and pictures.
- Concentrate as you read.

 Predict what this selection will be about. After reading, confirm or revise your prediction with your partner.

Respond and Extend: Venn Diagram

Compare Texts

Complete the Venn diagram to compare how treasure maps are used in the selections.

Venn Diagram

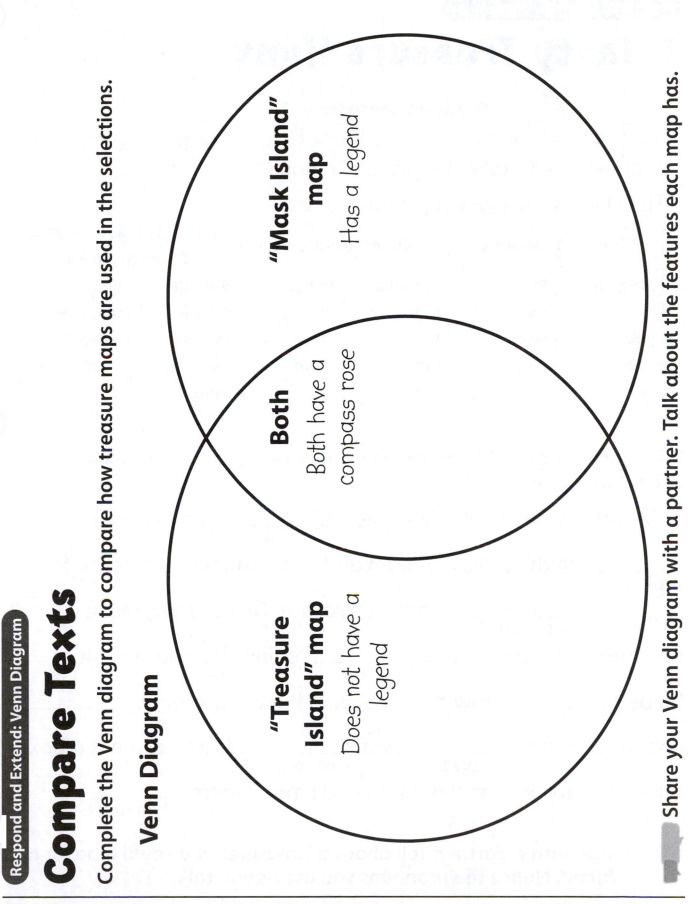

"Mask Island" map

Has a legend

Both

Both have a compass rose

"Treasure Island" map

Does not have a legend

Share your Venn diagram with a partner. Talk about the features each map has.

Name _____ Date _____

A Tasty Treasure Hunt

Grammar Rules Pronoun Agreement

A pronoun can take the place of a noun.

The chart shows which pronoun to use.

Subject Pronouns		Object Pronouns		Pronouns that Name the Same Noun Twice	
Singular	**Plural**	**Singular**	**Plural**	**Singular**	**Plural**
I	we	me	us	myself	ourselves
you	you	you	you	yourself	yourselves
she	they	her	them	herself	themselves
he		him		himself	
it		it		itself	

Read the paragraph. Replace the word or words under the line with the correct pronoun.

My little brother Jake likes pirates. ____He____ reads about
                                           Jake

_____ all the time. My mom and I are planning a surprise for
  pirates

_____ . _____ will hide a treasure. Then we will make a
  Jake   Mom and I

treasure map. Jake will use _____ to find the treasure. Mom
                                map

helped _____ draw the map. But I hid the present by _____ .
           I   I

I hope Jake shares _____ with _____ . The treasure is a box
                      present   Mom and me

full of his favorite cookies. Mom and I made them _____ .
                                                      Mom and I

💬 **Talk with a partner. Tell about a "treasure" you could hide for a friend. Notice the pronouns you use as you talk.**

Thinking Map: Time Line

Make a Time Line

Make a time line to show the steps you took to find a lost object.

Time Line

✂ Use your time line to tell a partner about your search for a lost object.

Grammar: Possessive Pronouns

Our Hidden Treasure

Grammar Rules Possessive Pronouns

A possessive pronoun takes the place of a person's name and what the person owns.

Singular	Plural
mine, yours, his, hers	ours, yours, theirs

Read the play. Complete the dialogue with the possessive pronoun that takes the place of the underlined words.

AIESHA: We need <u>your treasure map</u>, Daanish. Can you find
___yours___ ?

DAANISH: No, and the pirates have _____ . They might follow
<u>their map</u> to our gold.

BAO: But Captain Bellamy lost _____ . <u>His treasure map</u>
sank with the ship.

AIESHA: Oh wait! I found _____ . We can follow <u>my map</u>.
(*The three children follow Aisha's map.*)

BAO: I think <u>our gold</u> is buried here. Dig! Soon it will be
_____ again!

💬 **Choose parts and read the play aloud.**

Name _____   Date _____

Real Pirates: The Untold Story of the Whydah

1
Barry Clifford was always fascinated by the story of the pirate ship Whydah. He and his crew began to search for the shipwreck.

2
The Whydah was originally a slave ship. It traveled from Europe to Africa to America, trading slaves for goods.

3
On its last trip, the Whydah left a Caribbean port loaded with treasure. Two pirate ships captured the Whydah. Later, the Whydah sank in a storm.

4
300 years later, Clifford and his crew found the shipwreck. They bring objects up from the ship. These objects tell about life on the Whydah. Many of the objects are on display.

▲ Objects from the wreck of the Whydah

Grammar: Demonstrative Pronouns

What Is This? What Is That?

Grammar Rules Demonstratives

A demonstrative pronoun refers to a specific noun without naming it.

For One: this, that	For More Than One: these, those
This is cargo. *That* is a map.	*These* are gold coins. *Those* are jewels.

Set Up the Game:

1. Form groups of 4 to 6 students. Divide each group into two teams.

2. Together, teams choose 10 or more Language Builder Picture Cards. About half of the cards should show one object. The other half should show more than one object.

> Those are bars of silver.

> This is a sailing ship.

Play:

3. Team One draws and displays a card from the deck. Team Two uses *that* or *those* to describe it.

4. Team Two draws a card, displays it, and uses *this* or *these* to describe it.

5. Team Two draws a card. Team One uses *that* or *those* to describe it.

6. Team One draws a card and uses *this* or *these* to describe it.

7. Continue playing until all of the cards have been used. If you wish, shuffle the deck and play again!

/HB

Around the World

1. Write each Key Word on your passport.

2. Wait until you are a traveler or a challenger.

3. Listen to a definition of a Key Word and try to be the first to name the word.

4. Check off each word that you correctly name.

5. Check off all the words in your passport or make it "Around the World," and you win!

Passport

☐ _____   ☐ _____

☐ _____   ☐ _____

☐ _____   ☐ _____

☐ _____   ☐ _____

☐ _____   ☐ _____

Name _____ Date _____

"Real Pirates"

Complete the time line to tell the sequence of events in "Real Pirates."

In 1715 the slave ship *Whydah* was built.

Captain Prince took the ship to Africa.

💬 Use your time line to retell the article to a partner.

Fluency: Phrasing

"Real Pirates"

Use this passage to practice reading with proper phrasing.

After capturing the *Whydah*, the pirates sailed north, robbing   9

more rich ships on the way.   15

Then the *Whydah* was struck by a storm off Cape Cod on   27

the night of April 26, 1717. Strong winds drove the *Whydah* onto   39

a sandbar just 500 feet from shore. The ship was slammed by   51

waves up to twenty feet high. Soon, the mainmast snapped.   61

The *Whydah* was pushed off the sandbar and capsized.   70

There were 145 men and at least one boy aboard the *Whydah*.   82

Only two made it to shore alive. The rest died in the dark, cold water.   97

The *Whydah's* riches quickly sank. They disappeared in the   106

shifting sands of the Cape. There they stayed for nearly three   117

hundred years.   119

From "Real Pirates," page 402

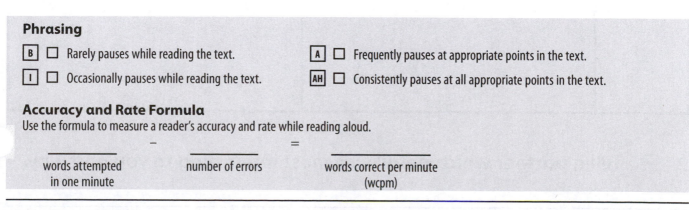

Phrasing

B ☐ Rarely pauses while reading the text.

I ☐ Occasionally pauses while reading the text.

A ☐ Frequently pauses at appropriate points in the text.

AH ☐ Consistently pauses at all appropriate points in the text.

Accuracy and Rate Formula

Use the formula to measure a reader's accuracy and rate while reading aloud.

_____	−	_____	=	_____
words attempted in one minute		number of errors		words correct per minute (wcpm)

©/HB

Name _____   Date _____

"La Belle Shipwreck"

Use the double-entry log to record what you read and your ideas about it.

Page	What I Read	What It Means to Me

Tell a partner which detail was most interesting to you and why.

Name _____ Date _____

Compare Media Texts

Use the comparison chart to compare "La Belle Shipwreck" to a blog.

Feature	Web article	Blog
Title	"La Belle Shipwreck"	
Name of author	Texas Beyond History	
Date when written?	no	
Is the text in sections?		
Are there pictures?		
Does the information change often?		
Are there mostly facts or mostly opinions?		
Are there links to other articles and websites or definitions?		

💬 Take turns with a partner. Ask each other questions about the features of Web articles and blogs.

Grammar: Possessive Pronouns

The Treasure Is Yours

Grammar Rules Possessive Pronouns

Use **possessive pronouns** to show that someone owns something.

Possessive Pronouns	mine	yours	his	hers	ours	theirs

A possessive pronoun does not come before a noun.

A possessive pronoun stands alone.

Answer each question with a possessive pronoun.

1. Are these their ships?   No, the ships are not __theirs__.

2. Is this La Salle's ship?   Yes, this ship is _____.

3. Is this our shipwreck?   Yes, this shipwreck is _____.

4. Is this the woman's shoe?   Yes, this shoe is _____.

5. Are these your tools?   No, those tools are _____.

6. Is that your treasure?   Yes, this treasure is _____.

Ask a partner questions about classroom objects. Use language frames: Whose _____ is this? Whose _____ are these? Have your partner use possessive pronouns to answer the questions. Then switch roles.

Name _____   Date _____

Focus and Coherence

	How do the events fit with each other?	How complete is the writing?
4 Wow!	• The plot is clear. • All the events and characters fit and make sense for the plot.	• The writing feels complete. • The story has a clear beginning, middle, and end.
3 Ahh.	• The plot is fairly clear. • Most of the events and characters fit and make sense for the plot.	• The writing feels mostly complete. • Parts of the beginning, middle, and end are clear.
2 Hmm.	• The plot is somewhat clear. • Some of the events and characters fit and make sense for the plot.	• The writing feels somewhat complete. • The beginning, middle, and end are not all clear.
1 Huh?	• The plot is difficult to understand. • Few of the events and characters fit and make sense for the plot.	• The writing feels incomplete. • The story has no beginning, middle, or end. It just has a few events.

Name _____ Date _____

Character Map

Complete the Character Map for your historical fiction story.

Events	Relationships

Character: _____

Beginning	Middle	End

Name _____   Date _____

Revise

Use the Revising Marks to revise these paragraphs. Look for:

- **facts that are not accurate**
- **unrelated details**

Revising Marks

∧	Add.
℘	Take out.
⬭⟶	Move to here.
⬭	Check spelling.
⏋	Indent.

Maria raced down the stairs. She remembered a show she had seen on television. A person on a ship had hidden in a little cabinet in the ship's galley. Maria had to grab the map and try. She could hear the pirates and sailors fighting on the deck.

Maria reached for the map and shoved it under her shawl. Then she dashed to the galley. A galley is a kitchen on a ship. Maria ran into the galley and squeezed into the tiny cabinet by the dishwasher.

HB

©

Writing Project

Edit and Proofread

Use the Editing Marks to edit and proofread this paragraph. Look for:

- **pronoun agreement**
- **commas with introductory words and phrases**
- **correct use of: their/there/they're, it's/its, you're/your**

Editing Marks

⬭	Check spelling
℘	Take out

Right away Maria saw the pirates. She couldn't stop himself from shaking. "Put down you're weapons!" yelled the pirate. " Its time to give up!"

Name _____ Date _____

Moving Through Space

**Make a concept map with the answers to the Big Question:
What does it take to explore space?**

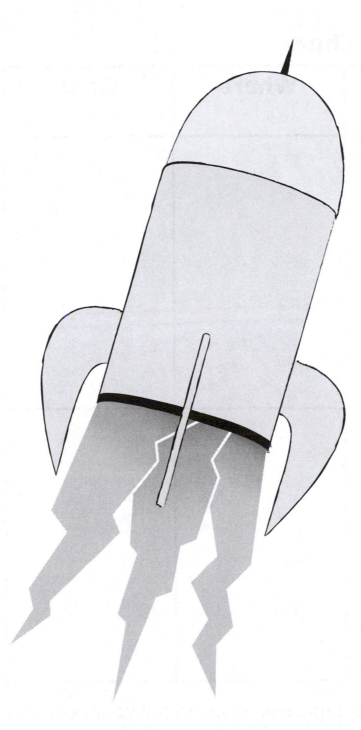

Name _____ Date _____

Comparing Sports

Make a comparison chart to compare one of the sports on page 427 with another sport.

Comparison Chart

Sport	Where	Goal	Measure Speed

Use your comparison chart to tell your partner about the two sports.

In the Dark Sky

Grammar Rules Adverbs

Adverbs often describe a verb. Adverbs usually answer one of these questions: *how? when?* or *where?*

How	When	Where
quietly slowly	soon yesterday	far there

Underline each adverb in the paragraph. Then categorize the adverbs.

<u>Yesterday</u>, Tana and I waited patiently for it to get dark outside. We had our telescope and our journals. Suddenly, it became dark. We eagerly looked through the telescope. I could see far into the sky. When I told Tana what I saw, she quickly took the telescope from me. The telescope made some items look as if they were nearby. Later, we wrote about our observations in our journals.

How	When	Where
_____	yesterday	_____
_____	_____	_____
_____	_____	_____

With a partner, ask and answer questions about exciting things you have seen. Use three adverbs from the chart.

Key Points Reading

What's Faster Than a Speeding Cheetah?

1

> ANIMAL SPEEDS
>
> human — 15
> ostrich — 45
> cheetah — 70
> peregrine falcon — 200
>
> 0   25   50   75   100   125   150   175   200
> Speed in Miles per Hour

An ostrich is faster than a human, but a cheetah is the world's fastest runner. A peregrine falcon is faster than a zooming car, but not as fast as an airplane.

2

> 150,000
> 25,000
> 1,300
>
> 0   25,000   50,000   75,000   100,000   125,000   150,000

Propeller planes are fast, but a jet plane can travel faster than the speed of sound. A rocket ship must go faster than a jet to make it into space. A space meteoroid goes six times faster than a rocket ship.

3

Yet, there is something even faster than a meteoroid. It is light. Light travels 299,338 kilometers per second. At that speed, you could circle the Earth more than seven times in one second. Most scientists believe nothing travels through space faster than light.

HB

©

Name _____   Date _____

The Adverb Game

Grammar Rules Comparing with Adverbs

Some adverbs can be used to describe and compare actions.

- Add **-er** to compare two actions. Add **-est** to compare three or more actions.

- If an adverb ends in **-ly,** use **more** or **less** to compare two actions. Use **the most** or **the least** to compare three or more actions.

1. Take turns in a small group.

2. Spin the spinner. Add *-er, -est, more, less, most,* or *least* to the adverb in a sentence. Use the new adverb to tell more about a verb.

Make a Spinner

1. Put a paper clip over center of the spinner.

2. Put the point of a pencil through the loop of the paper clip. Make sure the pencil goes through the paper.

3. Spin the paper clip to make a spinner.

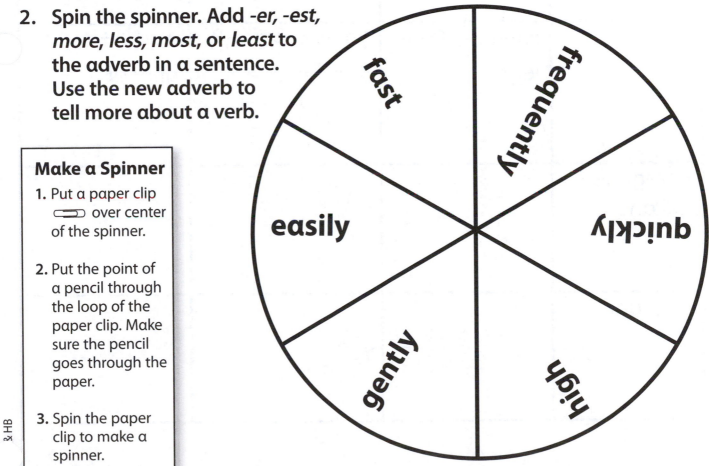

& HB
©

Reread and Compare: Comparison Chart

What's Faster Than a Speeding Cheetah?

Make a comparison chart for "What's Faster Than a Speeding Cheetah?"

Animal or Object	How It Moves	Fastest Speed	Record
ostrich	runs on two legs	24 km (15 mi) per hour	fastest animal with two legs
cheetah	runs on four legs	72 km (45 mi) per hour	fastest land animal
peregrine falcon			
jet plane			

HB

Use your comparison chart to tell a partner how the animals and objects are alike and different.

Fluency: Intonation

What's Faster Than a Speeding Cheetah?

Intonation is the rise and fall in the pitch or tone of your voice as you read aloud. Use this passage to practice reading with proper intonation.

Hold on a minute. There's something much faster than even	10
the fastest meteoroid. It's something you see all the time.	20
Just push the switch on a flashlight. Instantly, a light beam	31
will flash out at the amazing speed of 299,338 kilometers per	42
second (186,000 miles per second).	47
That's thousands of times faster than a meteoroid. At that speed,	58
a beam of light could circle Earth more than seven times in one second.	72
Most scientists believe that nothing can travel through space	81
faster than light. Who would have thought that the fastest traveling	92
thing in the whole universe could come out of something small	103
enough to hold in your hand?	109

From "What's Faster Than a Speeding Cheetah?" pages 440–441.

Intonation

| B | ☐ Does not change pitch. |
| I | ☐ Changes pitch, but does not match content. |

| A | ☐ Changes pitch to match some of the content. |
| AH | ☐ Changes pitch to match all of the content. |

Accuracy and Rate Formula
Use the formula to measure a reader's accuracy and rate when reading aloud.

$$\underline{\hspace{3cm}} \quad - \quad \underline{\hspace{3cm}} \quad = \quad \underline{\hspace{3cm}}$$

| words attempted in one minute | number of errors | words correct per minute (wcpm) |

Name _____   Date _____

Building for Space Travel

Complete this chart as you read "Building for Space Travel."

What I think:	What do you think?
_____	_____
Page _____	_____
_____	_____
Page _____	_____
_____	_____
Page _____	_____
_____	_____

Talk with your partner. Which thoughts are the same? Which are different?

Name _____   Date _____

Compare Fact and Opinion

Compare facts and opinions in the two selections.

	Facts	Opinions
"What's Faster Than a Speeding Cheetah?"		A peregrine falcon is magnificent.
"Building for Space Travel"	Constance Adams helped design TransHAb.	

HB

© 🔲🔲 **Take turns with a partner. Ask each other questions about the facts and opinions found in the selections.**

Grammar: Adverbs

Exercising in Zero Gravity

Grammar Rules Adverbs

- **Use adverbs to describe and compare actions.**

Describe 1 action	soon	careful**ly**	
Compare 2 actions	soon**er**	more careful**ly** than	less careful**ly** than
Compare more than 2 actions	soon**est**	the most careful**ly**	the least careful**ly**

Read each sentence. Write the correct form of the adverb on the line.

1. Every day I enter the gym _____*sooner*_____ than my partner.
   (soon)

2. I walk in _____ than a gymnast.
   (eagerly)

3. I notice that the equipment is attached _____ .
   (securely)

4. At first, I ran the _____ of all the astronauts.
   (quickly)

5. If I keep practicing, I may one day run the _____ of all.
   (fast)

6. Scientists planned TransHab the _____ of any gym.
   (carefully)

Pantomime an action an astronaut might do in zero gravity. Have your partner describe or compare your action using an adverb. Then switch roles.

Name _____ Date _____

Plot of a Story

Make a plot diagram about a favorite story.

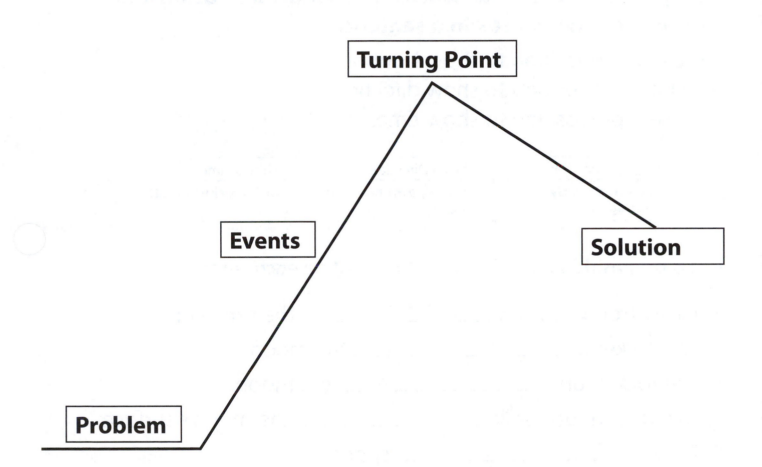

Turning Point

Events

Solution

Problem

💬 **Use the plot diagram to retell your story to a partner.**

Grammar: Prepositions

Moon Walk

Grammar Rules Prepositions

Prepositions are small words. They show a relationship between other words in a sentence.

- Use a preposition to show location.
- Use a preposition to show direction.
- Use a preposition to show time.

Shows Location	Shows Direction	Shows Time
in, on, over, by, between	**to, into, around, across, toward**	**before, during, after**

Use a preposition from the chart to complete each sentence.

1. The astronauts train _____*before*_____ their mission.

2. The rocket flies _____ the moon.

3. The rocket lands _____ the moon.

4. Two astronauts walk _____ the moon's surface.

5. They see stars _____ space.

6. The astronauts wear special suits _____ the moon walk.

Tell a partner about a place you would like to explore or have explored. Use prepositions in sentences to tell about your exploration.

Name _____ Date _____

The Moon Over Star

In 1969, Mae was looking forward to astronauts landing on the moon. Gramps thought it was a waste of money. Mae and her cousins watched the *Eagle* land, but Gramps kept working on his tractor.

Gramps wondered why money was spent on a trip to the moon. There were so many people on Earth who needed help. Mae wondered what Gramps' dreams were. She realized that Gramps was tired from working hard all his life.

Neil Armstrong walked on the moon. People all over the world were listening when he said, "That's one small step for man, one giant leap for mankind." Gramps said it was something to remember. He told Mae to keep dreaming.

Name _____   Date _____

Is That So? Tell Me More!

Grammar Rules Prepositional Phrases

1. Play with a partner.

2. Choose a picture from a magazine. Write your sentence as a caption.

3. Take turns building a related sentence with prepositional phrases. See how many you can use.

I see a boy. I see a boy **in a field**. I see a boy in a field **with a rocket**.

Paste your picture here.

Caption:

_____

_____

_____

Name _____ Date _____

Reread and Retell: Plot Diagram

The Moon Over Star

Make a plot diagram of "The Moon Over Star."

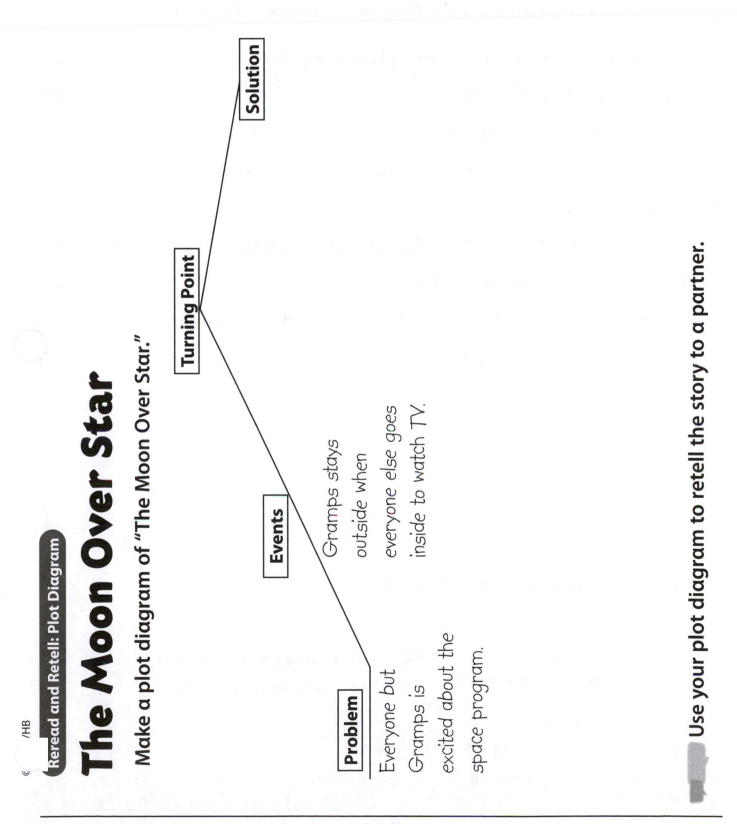

Problem

Everyone but
Gramps is
excited about the
space program.

Events

Gramps stays
outside when
everyone else goes
inside to watch TV.

Turning Point

Solution

Use your plot diagram to retell the story to a partner.

Fluency: Expression

"The Moon Over Star"

Use this passage to practice reading with proper expression.

Later, when it was as quiet as the world ever gets, Gramps	12
and I stood together under the moon.	19
"What's mankind?" I asked him.	24
"It's all of us," he finally said. "It's all of us who've ever lived,	38
all of us still to come."	44
I put my hand in his. "Just think, Gramps, if they could go	57
to the moon, maybe one day I could too!"	66
"Great days," he said, "an astronaut in the family. Who'd a thought?"	78
I smiled in the dark. My gramps was proud of me.	89

From "The Moon Over Star," page 473

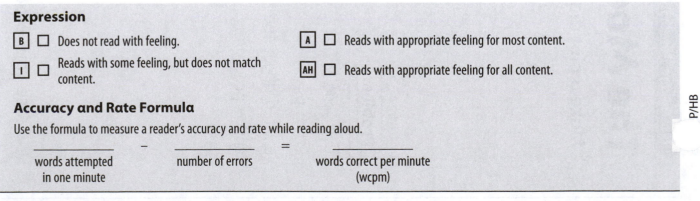

Expression

B ☐ Does not read with feeling.

I ☐ Reads with some feeling, but does not match content.

A ☐ Reads with appropriate feeling for most content.

AH ☐ Reads with appropriate feeling for all content.

Accuracy and Rate Formula

Use the formula to measure a reader's accuracy and rate while reading aloud.

_____ − _____ = _____
words attempted   number of errors   words correct per minute
in one minute   (wcpm)

P/HB

Name _____ Date _____

"The First Person on the Moon"

Fill in the fact notes with information about Neil Armstrong or the moon landing.

Amazing Fact

An amazing fact about _____

is _____

I found it in the selection _____

_____ _____
Name   Date

Amazing Fact

An amazing fact about _____

is _____

I found it in the selection _____

_____ _____
Name   Date

Amazing Fact

An amazing fact about _____

is _____

I found it in the selection _____

_____ _____
Name   Date

Work with a partner to share your facts. Take turns reading aloud your facts.

/HB

Compare Fiction and Biography

Compare a story and a biography.

Event or Fact	"The Moon Over Star"	"The First Person on the Moon"
Neil Armstrong was born in 1930.		✓
In 1961, President Kennedy said that America would send people to the moon.	✓	✓
Armstrong, Aldrin, and Collins flew to the moon in the summer of 1969.		
Armstrong was the commander of the mission.		
The first person to walk on the moon was Armstrong.		
The world watched on television.		
Armstrong said, "One small step for man, one giant leap for mankind."		
The astronauts placed a flag on the moon.		
The moon is 240,000 miles from Earth.		

Work with a partner to complete the chart. What other fact or event did you add? Discuss with another team the facts that each selection gave about Armstrong.

Name _____ Date _____

The Moon Over Me

Grammar Rules Prepositional Phrases

A prepositional phrase starts with a preposition and ends with a noun or a pronoun. A prepositional phrase can:

show where	in, on, at, over, under, above, below, next to, beside, in front of, behind
show time	after, until, before, during
show direction	into, throughout, up, down, through, across, to
add details	with, to, about , among, except, of, from

Add one or more prepositional phrases to each sentence.

1. I found a book about the moon _____.

2. The book was filled _____.

3. I was excited to take the book _____.

4. We have been studying _____.

5. My teacher liked the fact sheet _____.

6. My favorite photo is the picture _____.

HB

© 　　　　 **Choose a Picture Card and use prepositional phrases to tell about it. For example: I want to travel in a space ship.**

Voice and Style

	Does the writing sound real and unique to the writer?	How interesting are the words and sentences?
4 **Wow!**	• The writing sounds real and personal, as if the writer is talking right to me.	• The writer uses words and sentences that fit the audience and purpose.
3 **Ahh.**	• Most of the writing sounds real and personal, as if the writer is talking to me.	• The writer uses good words and sentences for the audience and purpose.
2 **Hmm.**	• Some of the writing sounds real and personal, but the writer doesn't seem to be talking to me.	• The writer uses some words and sentences that fit the audience and purpose.
1 **Huh?**	• None of the writing sounds real and personal. • I can't tell who the writer is.	• The words and sentences don't fit the audience and purpose. • The sentences do not have variety. They do not flow together well.

Name _____ Date _____

Comparison Chart

Complete the comparison chart for your personal narrative.

Before	During	After

HB

©

7.21

Revise

Use the Revising Marks to revise this passage. Look for:

- varied sentences types and lengths
- personal voice
- dialogue

Revising Marks

∧	Add.
℘	Take out.

Fast Isn't Always Best

After school my brother and I did our homework. I worked slowly. I took my time. I read the directions. I thought about what to write.

My brother worked quickly. My brother scribbled furiously. My mother told him to slow down. My mother told him to do his work carefully.

But my brother said loudly that he was done. He rushed outside. I was upset. I wanted to play outside too.

The next day I proudly showed my mother my papers. The teacher had written a nice comment on my story.

My brother's teacher had asked him to do his homework again. I learned that being the fastest doesn't always mean you are the best.

© & HB

Writing Project

Edit and Proofread

Use the Editing Marks to edit and proofread this passage. Look for:

- **spelling of adverb suffixes**

- **punctuation of dialogue**

- **adverbs and prepositional phrases**

Editing Marks

∧	Add.
℘	Take out.
⟳	Move to here.

Swim season was almost over. You alway win, said my friend Ryan. You're like a dolphin.

I confident stepped off the platform. I waited patient for the whistle. No one can beat me, I thought to myself. Suddenly, the whistle blew and I dove into the pool.

I took an early lead. I won't have to work hard very to win, I thought.

When I touched the edge of the pool, I was extreme shocked to see the coach happyily giving Ryan a high-five.

What happened?, I asked.

Ryan beat you, said Coach Harris. He's been practicing and training to get faster.

At that moment, I realized that being the fastest swimmer requires a lot of hard work.

Name _____ Date _____

Moon Over Star ("Mae on the Moon")

Setting: The play takes place at Mae's grandparents' house.

Cast of Characters: Narrator, Mae, Lacey, Carrie, Gran, Gramps

Scene 1: In Gran's garden

Mae, Lacey, and Carrie are standing next to a cardboard cutout of a spaceship.

Narrator: It was the summer of 1969. Everyone in Mae's family was excited—a man was going to the moon for the first time. Mae and her cousins pretended that they were going to the moon, too.

Mae *[in an official-sounding voice]*: Five…four…three…two…one…zero… liftoff!

Lacey *[jumping up and down]*: Liftoff! Liftoff! We're going to the moon!

Carrie *[dreamy]*: All the way to the moon… I wonder how far it is from us.

Mae: It's about 240,000 miles away. Some scientists say it's moving an inch or so away from us every year.

Gran calls from the house.

Gran *[excited]*: Come quick, everyone! They're landing on the moon!

The children run toward Gran, talking at the same time.

Narrator: The whole family sat in front of the TV, watching as the spaceship landed. But Gramps didn't come. He was working in the barn. Mae wondered why he wasn't interested in the moon landing.

Scene 2: On the porch

The sun is setting. Gramps is sitting in a chair, his feet stretched out in front of him. Mae is standing next to him. She's wearing his muddy work boots.

Mae: Gramps, will you watch the moon walk with me tonight?

Gramps: I'm very tired today, but maybe.

Mae: That's all right, Gramps. It's okay.

Narrator: Mae realized that he had been tired for a long time. She wondered what his dreams were. Later, the whole family watched the moon walk together.

Scene 3: On the porch

It's nighttime. Mae is standing just in front of the porch, looking up at the sky. Gramps walks up to Mae and puts his hand on her shoulder.

Gramps: That was something to remember, wasn't it?

Mae: It sure was! Gramps, what does "mankind" mean?

Gramps: It means all of us who ever lived, and all of us to come.

Gramps hugs Mae.

Mae: Gramps, just think. If they could go to the moon, I could too!

Gramps: You know, the very first airplane I ever saw was right over there. *[He points offstage.]* You keep on dreaming, Mae. Remember that we're here now together on the prettiest star in the heavens.

Narrator: Gramps had spent his whole life looking at the moon. It told him when to plant and when to harvest. And one summer night, it told Mae to dream.

End of play

Unit Concept Map

Saving a Piece of the World

Make a concept map with the answers to the Big Question: What's worth protecting?

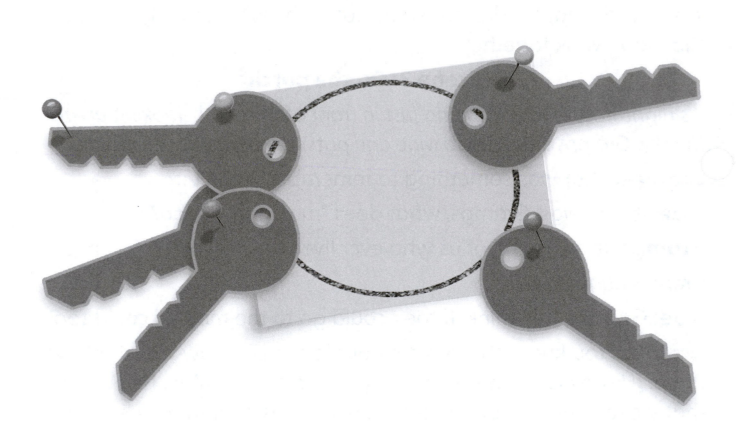

© & HB

Thinking Map: Goal and Outcome

Mapping a Goal

Make a goal-and-outcome map about a project that you completed.

Goal-and-Outcome Map

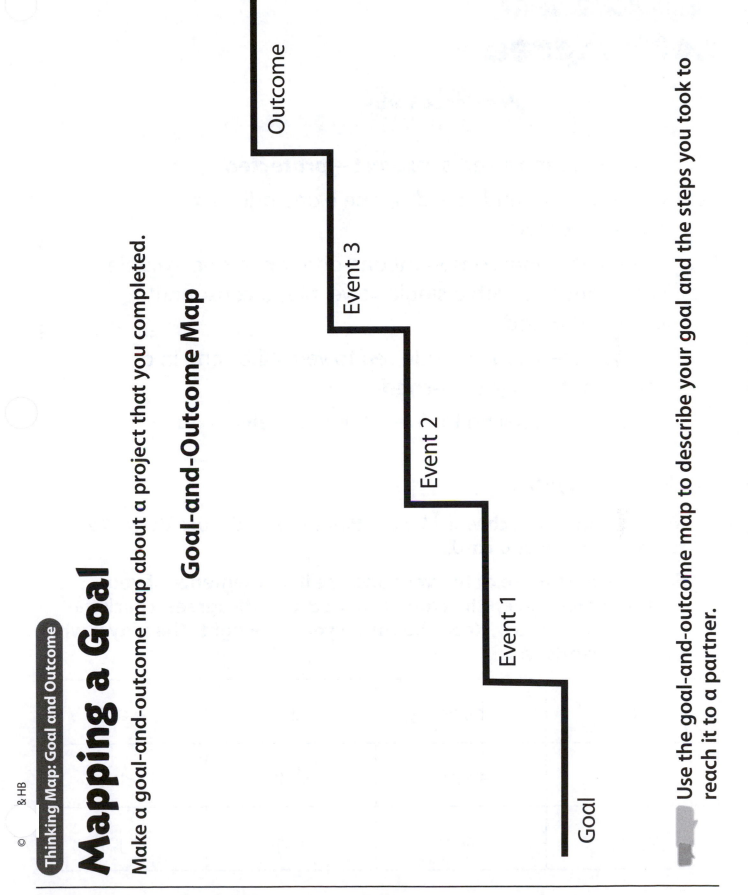

Outcome

Event 3

Event 2

Event 1

Goal

Use the goal-and-outcome map to describe your goal and the steps you took to reach it to a partner.

Grammar: Past-Tense Verbs

Let's Agree

Grammar Rules Past-Tense Verbs

1. Add -**ed** to most verbs. **protect—protected**

2. For verbs that end in **e**, drop the **e** and add -**ed**. **value—valued**

3. Double the final consonant and add -**ed** to one-syllable verbs that end with a single vowel plus a consonant. **plan—planned**

4. Change the **y** to **i** and add -**ed** to verbs that end in a consonant plus **y**. **try—tried**

5. Change the spelling for irregular verbs. **give—gave**

1. **Play with a partner.**

2. **Make a card for each word below. Place the cards face down. Take turns turning over a card.**

3. **Spell the past tense of the verb and use it in a sentence. If your partner agrees, keep the card. If your partner disagrees, check the word in a dictionary. Keep the card if you were right. The player with the most cards wins.**

clap	hope	do	walk
go	spend	stop	reply
hurry	save	keep	enjoy

& HB

©

Name _____   Date _____

Buffalo Music

1  Molly lived in Palo Duro Canyon in Texas. As she did her chores, she listened to the sounds of the buffalo moving through the canyon. She called it buffalo music.

2 One day, Molly heard gunshots in the canyon. Hunters were killing the buffalo for their hides and hooves. Six seasons later, the hunters were gone. So was the buffalo music.

3  A neighbor brought two orphaned buffalo calves to Molly. Molly wanted to help them because she didn't want all the buffalo to disappear.
Soon many people brought her orphans. Her herd grew to one hundred animals.

4  Molly heard that Yellowstone National Park wanted to make its buffalo herd bigger. She sent four buffalo to Yellowstone on a train.
The sounds of the canyon are different now, but she can still remember the faint sounds of the buffalo music.

© &HB

Grammar: Present-Perfect Tense

When Did It Happen?

Grammar Rules Present-Perfect Tense

- Use the past tense if you know when an action happened.
- Use the present-perfect tense if you don't know when a past action happened.
- Use the present-perfect tense if a past action is still happening.
- To form the present perfect, use **has** or **have** and a main verb.

Read each sentence. Underline the correct form of the verb.

1. People (hunted/<u>have hunted</u>) animals throughout history.

2. During the late 1800s, people (hunted/have hunted) bison to near extinction.

3. One spring, Molly (received/has received) two orphaned calves.

4. She (worked/has worked) through the summer to save them.

5. Life in the canyon (changed/has changed) over time.

6. Recent settlers made/have made Palo Duro Canyon a different place.

Talk with a partner about things you have done. Use the past tense and the present-perfect tense in your sentences.

© _____ & HB

Buffalo Music

Make a goal-and-outcome map for "Buffalo Music."

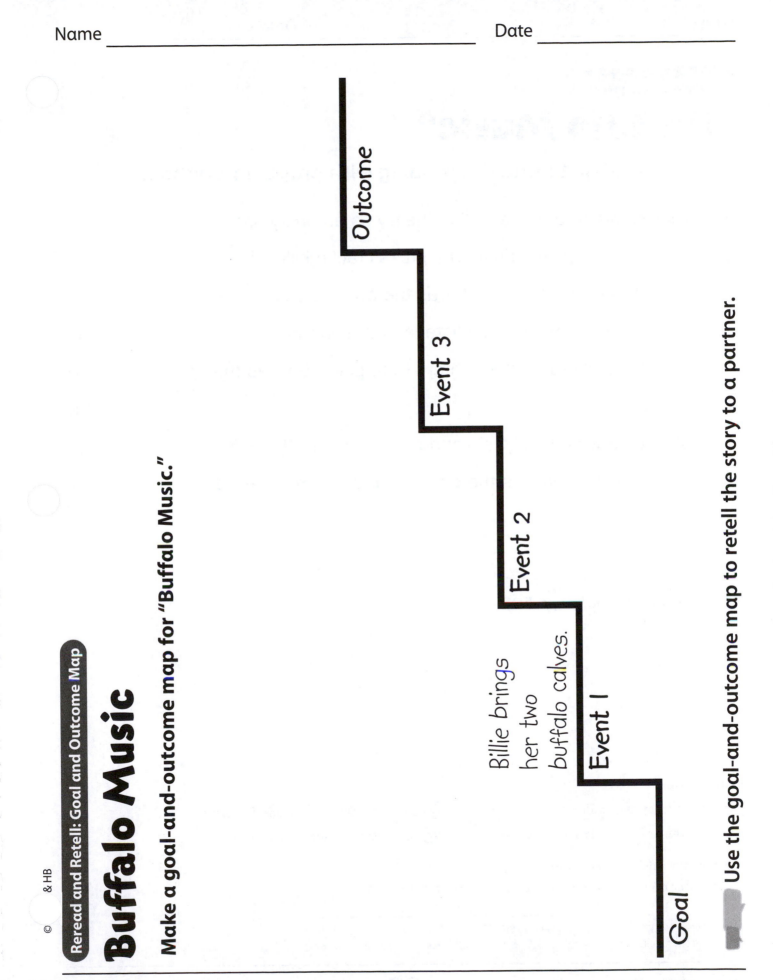

Outcome

Event 3

Event 2

Billie brings her two buffalo calves.

Event 1

Goal

Use the goal-and-outcome map to retell the story to a partner.

"Buffalo Music"

Use this passage to practice reading with proper intonation.

That summer, the heat fell as heavy as an angry fist.   11

The trails were deep with dust. The grass cracked like glass   22

underfoot. And everywhere, as far as the eye could see, the   33

bleached bones of the buffalo glistened white in the sun.   43

Within six seasons, the hunters were gone. So was the   53

buffalo music.   55

Oh, those were lonely, silent days! I was sure the only   66

song left in the canyon was the old whistle of the north wind.   79

From "Buffalo Music" page 502.

Intonation

| B | ☐ Does not change pitch. | A | ☐ Changes pitch to match some of the content. |
| I | ☐ Changes pitch, but does not match content. | AH | ☐ Changes pitch to match all of the content. |

Accuracy and Rate Formula

Use the formula to measure a reader's accuracy and rate while reading aloud.

_____   –   _____   =   _____

words attempted   number of errors   words correct per minute
in one minute   (wcpm)

Name _____ Date _____

Saving Bison From Extinction

Fill in the K-W-L-Q chart as you read the selection. Start with What I Know and move across the rows.

K What I Know	W What I Want To Know	L What I Learned	Q Questions I Still Have

Talk with a partner about where you might find answers to the questions you still have.

Compare Fiction and Nonfiction

Make a Venn Diagram to compare a fiction selection and a nonfiction selection.

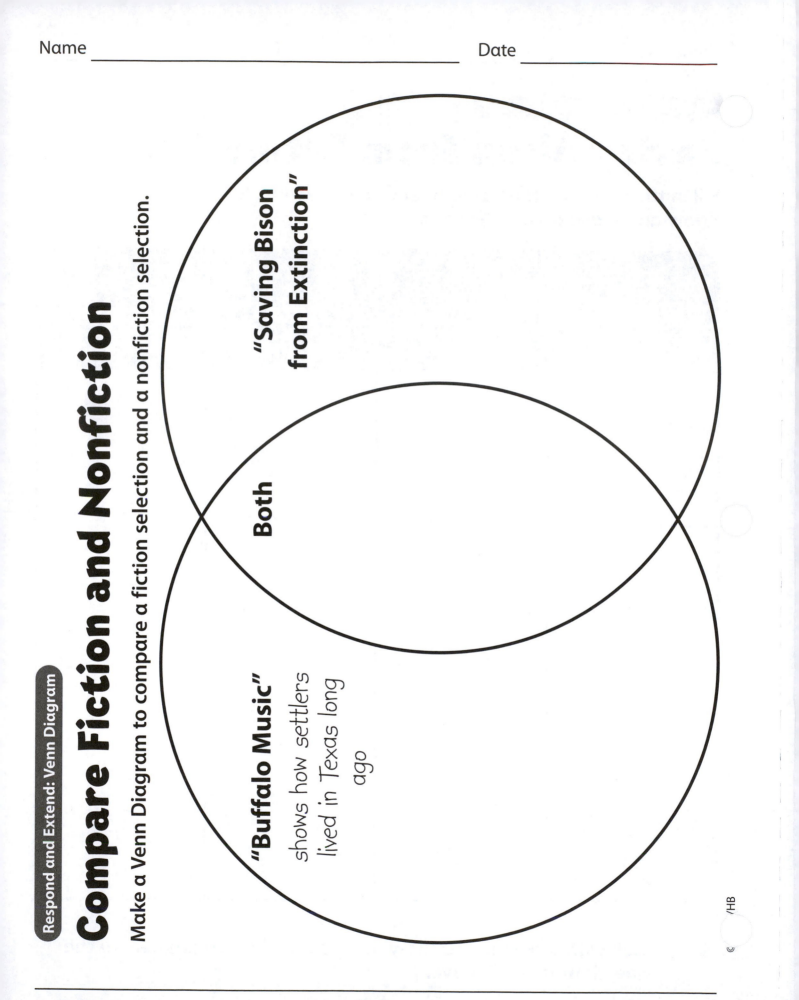

"Saving Bison from Extinction"

Both

"Buffalo Music"
shows how settlers lived in Texas long ago

Grammar: Past Tense

In the Past

Grammar Rules Past Tense

- Add **-ed** to form the past tense of most verbs.
- Drop the final **e** and add **-ed** to verbs like *live* (**lived**).
- Double the final consonant and add **-ed** to verbs like *hop* (**hopped**).
- Change the **y** to **i** and add **-ed** to verbs like *cry* (**cried**).
- Learn the special past-tense forms of irregular verbs like *come* (**came**) and *have* (**had**).

Write the past tense form of the verb to complete each sentence.

Samuel Walking Coyote was a Native American who _____ to
(help)

protect the bison. One day, several orphaned calves _____ into his
(walk)

camp. Walking Coyote _____ the orphaned calves. Soon, his small
(raise)

herd _____ . He _____ his herd to people who _____ to let
(grow)   (sell)   (plan)

the bison roam free. William Hornaday _____ to protect the bison,
(try)

too. Hornaday _____ a small group of bison to the Bronx Zoo. He
(bring)

_____ the bison from becoming extinct by forming the American
(saved)

Bison Society.

**With your partner, write a paragraph to tell how bison were almost
hunted to extinction. Use past tense verbs in your sentences.**

Name _____   Date _____

Analyze a Message

Make a fact-and-opinion chart about an ad, poster, or flyer you have seen.

Facts	Opinions

/HB

Grammar: Past Progressive

The Q and A Game

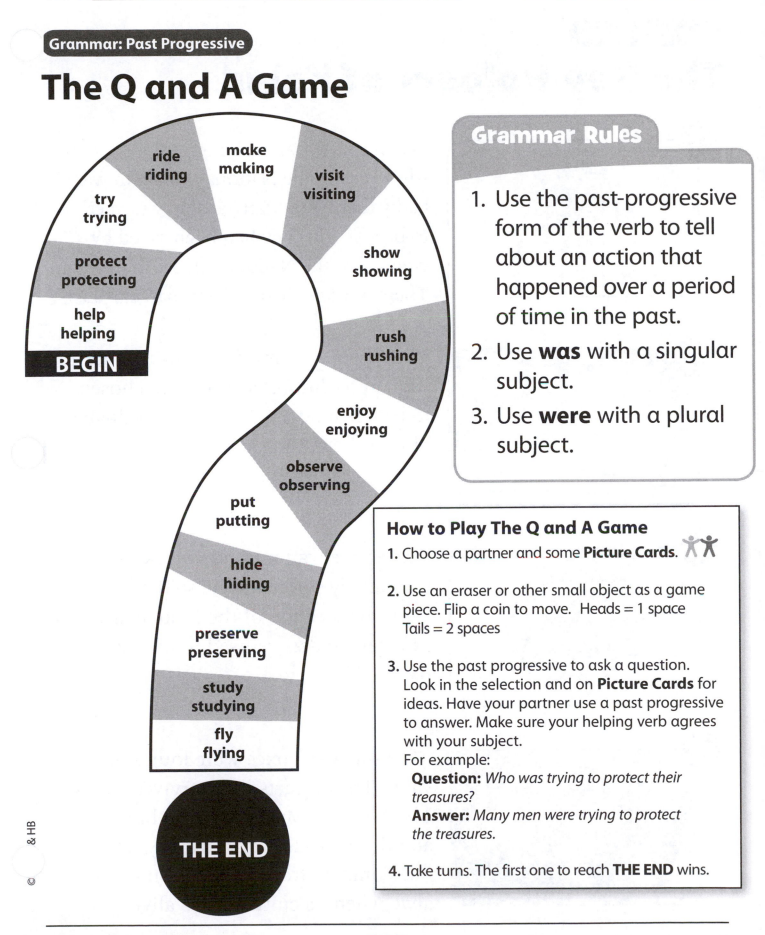

ride
riding

make
making

visit
visiting

try
trying

show
showing

protect
protecting

help
helping

BEGIN

rush
rushing

enjoy
enjoying

observe
observing

put
putting

hide
hiding

preserve
preserving

study
studying

fly
flying

THE END

Grammar Rules

1. Use the past-progressive form of the verb to tell about an action that happened over a period of time in the past.

2. Use **was** with a singular subject.

3. Use **were** with a plural subject.

How to Play The Q and A Game

1. Choose a partner and some **Picture Cards**.

2. Use an eraser or other small object as a game piece. Flip a coin to move. Heads = 1 space Tails = 2 spaces

3. Use the past progressive to ask a question. Look in the selection and on **Picture Cards** for ideas. Have your partner use a past progressive to answer. Make sure your helping verb agrees with your subject.
   For example:
   Question: *Who was trying to protect their treasures?*
   Answer: *Many men were trying to protect the treasures.*

4. Take turns. The first one to reach **THE END** wins.

© & HB

Name _____   Date _____

The Key Holders of Kabul

1  When a civil war broke out in Afghanistan, the National Museum was badly damaged. Many artifacts seemed to be lost. But they had been saved by workers at the National Museum in Kabul. These workers had hidden many artifacts.

2  The museum workers follow an ancient Afghan tradition. Workers are chosen to be key holders. They guard valuable objects.

3  During the war, museum workers were arrested by soldiers. The soldiers tried to learn the location of the hidden artifacts. The key holders refused to betray their national history.

4  After the war, boxes were found inside a vault. The artifacts had survived the war. The National Museum was rebuilt and the artifacts are on display. The museum's mottos is: "A nation stays alive when its culture stays alive.

Name _____   Date _____

What Will You Do?

Grammar Rules Future Tense

1. Use **will** plus a main verb to tell about a future action.

   I will visit a museum with my fourth-grade class.

2. You can also use **am going to, is going to,** or **are going to,** plus a main verb to tell about a future action.

   We are going to look at objects from the Civil War.

   Our teacher is going to explain the artifacts to us.

   I am going to bring my camera and take pictures.

Choose a place you would like to visit to learn about the past. Write future tense sentences to tell about what you will see or do. Include both ways of telling about the future.

_____

_____

_____

_____

_____

_____

_____

Share your sentences with a partner. Check each others' sentences to make sure that the future tense was used correctly.

Vocabulary: Apply Word Knowledge

Vocabulary Bingo

1. Write one Key Word next to each key.

2. Listen to the clues. Find the Key Word and use a marker to cover it.

3. Say "Bingo" when you have four markers in a row.

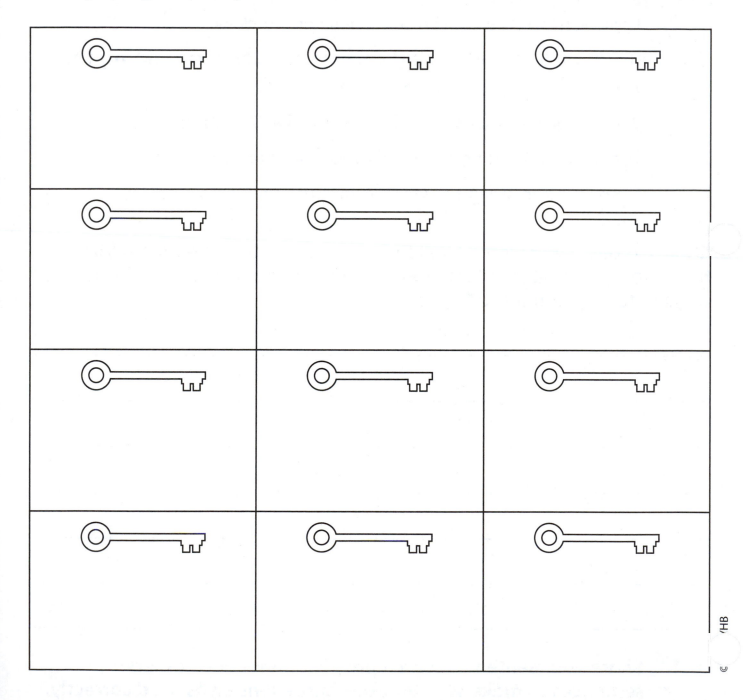

The Key Holders of Kabul

Complete a fact-and-opinion chart about "The Key Holders of Kabul."

Facts	Opinions
In 1987, I went to Central Asia.	After hearing Sarianidi's story, I knew the objects he had found were remarkable.

© **Use your fact-and-opinion chart to analyze the personal narrative for your partner.**

HB

Fluency: Phrasing

The Key Holders of Kabul

Use this passage to practice reading with appropriate phrasing.

In 1979, the Soviet Union invaded Afghanistan. Sarianidi wanted	9
to protect the treasures he had uncovered. Secretly, he moved them	20
to the National Museum in Kabul.	26
The fight against the Soviets became a civil war. Within two years,	38
a museum in another Afghan city was robbed. Workers at the National	50
Museum did not want their treasures to be lost, too.	60
In 1988, the museum key holders in Kabul packed and labeled	71
their most valuable objects. They hid them in a vault in the presidential	84
palace in Kabul. The key holders kept their secret well. The Afghan	96
people and the rest of the world believed the artifacts had disappeared.	108

From "The Key Holders of Kabul," page 541

Phrasing

| B | ☐ Rarely pauses while reading the text. | A | ☐ Frequently pauses at appropriate points in the text. |
| I | ☐ Occasionally pauses while reading the text. | AH | ☐ Consistently pauses at all appropriate points in the text. |

Accuracy and Rate Formula

Use the formula to measure a reader's accuracy and rate while reading aloud.

_____   −   _____   =   _____

words attempted   number of errors   words correct per minute
in one minute   (wcpm)

Name _____ Date _____

The Librarian of Basra

Complete a reflection journal as you read "The Librarian of Basra."

Page	What I Read	What It Means to Me

💬 **Compare journals with someone you have not worked with today. See if you asked any of the same questions. If so, discuss your answers. If not, take turns explaining why you asked each question.**

HB
©

Compare Features

Make a comparison chart to compare features of an informational text and a literary text.

	"The Key Holders of Kabul"	"The Librarian of Basra"
genre	personal narrative	
real or fiction?	real	
text features	photographs	
point of view		
author's purpose		
how you know the purpose		

8.19

Name _____   Date _____

A Library in Your Future

Grammar Future Tense

1. Use the helping verb **will** along with a main verb.

   Our library **will move** to a bigger building.

2. Use **am going to, is going to,** or **are going to** with a main verb.

   I **am going to like** the new building.

   It **is going to have** room for more books.

   Officials **are going to offer** more programs.

Complete each sentence with the future tense. Use the main verb in parentheses.

1. The library __will extend__ its hours.
   (extend)

2. It _____ early on Saturdays.
   (open)

3. Two teachers _____ there after school.
   (work)

4. They _____ students with their homework.
   (help)

5. The librarian _____ a movie section.
   (offer)

6. You _____ movies just like you do books!
   (borrow)

7. I _____ the new computers.
   (enjoy)

> **Talk with a partner about the larger library. What else will people be able to do there?**

¿HB?

© I

Name _____   Date _____

Organization

	Is the writing organized?	Does the writing flow?
4 **Wow!**	• The writing is organized. It fits the writer's purpose.	• The writing is very smooth. Each idea flows into the next one.
3 **Ahh.**	• The writing is mostly organized. It fits the writer's purpose.	• The writing is pretty smooth. There are only a few places where it jumps around.
2 **Hmm.**	• The writing is organized, but it doesn't fit the writer's purpose.	• The writing jumps from one idea to another idea, but I can still follow it a little.
1 **Huh?**	• The writing is not organized. Maybe the writer forgot to use a chart to plan.	• I can't tell what the writer wants to say.

T-Chart

Complete the T-Chart for your literary response.

What I Liked	What I Didn't Like

HB

©

Revise

Use the Revising Marks to revise these paragraphs. Look for:

- a short summary of the literature
- a clearly stated opinion
- reasons that support the opinion
- details that help develop ideas.

Revising Marks	
∧	Add.
℘	Take out.
⌒⟋	Move to here.

"A Million Trees"
by Beatriz
Reviewed by Latifah Malouf

"A Million Trees" is a poem written by Beatriz, a student like us, to tell one thing she can do to save a piece of the earth. I liked this poem but I wish it was longer.

I am worried about pollution. The reason Beatriz gave for planting trees. She said, "The trees will be of service. The air will be much cleaner."

The poem was fun to read. I liked the rhyme and the images it made in my mind. The squirrels will adore it.

Name _____ Date _____

Edit and Proofread

Use the Editing Marks to edit and proofread this passage. Look for:

- suffixes and base words
- regular and irregular past-tense verbs
- future tense
- punctuating titles

Editing Marks	
∧	Add.
℘	Take out.
⬭⟋	Move to here.
⬭	Check spelling.
≡	Capitalize.

This is one of the best articles I've read about a neighborhood environmental program. It made me want to start a program in my own neighborhood. I am especially interested when the author wrote, "My life and the lives of all my neighbors changeed after we began working together." The article made me hopful.

I felt really sad when I readed the writer's comments about huge amounts of waste. So, I will take her recommendation. I am go to read the article titled How to Start a recycling program in Your Own Neighborhood next week.

Last year, I carryed our neighborhood newspapers to the Recycling Center. The article made me feel proud because I goed with my entire family to get this done.

HB

©

Acknowledgments

Acknowledgments
Grateful acknowledgment is given to the authors, artists, photographers, museums, publishers, and agents for permission to reprint copyrighted material. Every effort has been made to secure the appropriate permission. If any omissions have been made or if corrections are required, please contact the Publisher.

Lerner Publishing Group, Inc.: *Love and Roast Chicken* by Barbara Knutson. Copyright © 2004 by Barbara Knutson. Reprinted with the permission of Carolrhoda Books, a division of Lerner Publishing Group, Inc. All rights reserved. No part of this excerpt may be used or reproduced in any manner whatsoever without the prior written permission of Lerner Publishing Group, Inc.

Farrar Straus & Giroux, LLC: *How I Learned Geography* by Uri Shulevitz. Copyright © 2008 by Uri Shulevitz. Reprinted by permission of Farrar, Straus and Giroux, LLC.

Random House, Inc.: *Doña Flor* by Pat Mora, illustrated by Raúl Colón. Text copyright © 2005 by Pat Mora. Illustrations © 2005 by Raúl Colón. Reprinted by permission of Random House, Inc.

Scholastic, Inc.: *The Fungus that Ate My School* by Arthur Dorros, illustrated by David Catrow. Illustrations © 2000 by David Catrow. Reprinted by permission of Scholastic Inc., Scholastic Press.

National Geographic Books: Adaptation from *Real Pirates: The Untold Story of the Whydah from Slave Ship to Pirate Ship* by Barry Clifford, illustrated by Gregory Manchess. Illustrations © 2008 by Gregory Manchess. Reprinted with permission.

Penguin Group (USA) Inc: *The Moon Over Star* by Diana Hutts Aston, illustrated by Jerry Pinkney. Illustrations © 2008 by Jerry Pinkney. Used by permission of Dial Books for Young Readers, a division of Penguin Young Readers Group, a member of Penguin Group (USA) Inc., 345 Hudson Street, New York, NY 10014. All rights reserved.

Photographs:
1.4 (all) Josh Ponte. **2.12** (1) Gorilla Foundation/AP Images, (2) Anup Shah/Nature Picture Library, (3)Mattias Klum/National Geographic Image Collection, (4) BIOS Bios - Auteurs Ruoso Cyril/Peter Arnold, Inc. **3.1** John Foxx Images/Imagestate. **3.13** (1) Warren Morgan/Corbis, (2) Yann Arthus-Bertrand/Corbis, (3) David Doubliet/National Geographic Image Collection, (4) Mark Cosslett/National Geographic Image Collection. **4.4** (3-l) Warren Faidley/Corbis, (3-r) Stocktrek/PhotoDisc/Getty Images. **4.17** Jim Cummins/Taxi/Getty Images. **5.1** Artville. **6.13** (1)Brian J. Skerry/National Geographic Image Collection, (4) Kenneth Garrett. **8.13** (1) Thierry Ollivier/Musee Guimet/Getty Images, (2) Amir Zia/AP Images, (3) Leonid Bogdanov/SuperStock, (4) Musadeq Sadeq/AP Images.

Illustrator Credits
Dartmouth Publishing, Inc.

The National Geographic Society
John M. Fahey, Jr., President & Chief Executive Officer
Gilbert M. Grosvenor, Chairman of the Board